TIED

TO

TERROR

SECRETS OF A BATTERED WIFE

TIED

TO

TERROR

SECRETS OF A BATTERED WIFE

J. HANNAH LLOYD

COMPANION TO
ESCAPE FROM ABUSE
SURVIVAL GUIDE

This book is a non-fiction memoir, and includes Bible references and scripture. Names and locations are simply products of the author's imagination. *Escape from Abuse Survival Guide* is the second book in this series.

Endorsements

My heart is on fire after reading J. Hannah Lloyd's exquisitely wrought narrative. She has put the religious world on notice that even a pastor's wife can suffer years of torture at the hands of a zealot husband.

With an original voice, *Tied to Terror-Secrets of a Battered Wife* is a startling account, a revelation of the sin embedded within a Christian man's soul. Battling her way out of the darkness, she emerged with her faith in tact; and walked into a life that was calling her name. And for this we give praise.

—Pamela King Cable
Author of *Televenge: the dark side of televangelism*

J. Hannah married young, with hopes and dreams of life as a pastor's wife. But within days she discovered her dream was a nightmare. With vivid detail and heart-wrenching transparency, the author takes readers behind the scenes of physical, emotional, and verbal abuse at the hands of a volatile man who was both pastor and evangelist.

But her story, *Tied to Terror-Secrets of a Battered wife*, is more than that of a battered wife. The author digs deep into her life, and peels back layers of childhood trauma, family loss, and health issues; then brings her story into an ending that is both revealing, and exquisitely glorious.

—Vonda Skelton
Author, *Seeing Through the Lies: Unmasking the Myths Women Believe*

J. Hannah Lloyd chronicles her life with an abusive husband and a chance at freedom with honest and clear writing. Throughout the story, she sprinkles Scripture verses that helped to keep her strong. She also shows how God is our strength, and our refuge.

Grab a tissue when you read *Tied to Terror-Secrets of a Battered Wife.*

—Pam Zollman
Author, speaker, freelance editor,
Writing Instructor

Dedicated to my husband—
the love of my life
and my children—
the delights of my life

Contents

Preface

When I fell in love at the age of nineteen, the future looked sunny and bright. My new husband was both charismatic and handsome; our marriage, a dream-come-true. But his representation as minister of the Gospel, devoted to both God and man, wasn't justified. The truth of reality would soon shatter my vision, innocence, and religious beliefs as I realized my jump from the frying pan into the fire was a horrible mistake.

Although misguided, I was committed, and worked diligently to make the marriage a success. But inner turmoil, the result of assaults, insults, and battering began to slaughter the love I once had for my husband. Yet I remained true to my marriage vows.

What goes on in a marriage behind closed doors is nobody's business. But when the truth is revealed, families often refuse to believe their loved one is an abuser—or married to one.

For most, family is where one goes when bruised and battered. But not mine. The embarrassment I felt disguised what appeared to be a marriage made in heaven. My reality remained hidden behind a façade of family disregard, church ineptness, and an overall lack of perception.

Love hurts, but shouldn't. Yet from the pit of despair, a thread of hope for deliverance was born. Still it required twelve years of deception to unravel all the disillusionment, heartache, and despair that long played havoc with my sanity.

But after years of unrestrained cruelty, the facts of realism began forcing the light of truth to shine at the end of a compelling tunnel. Misery was then replaced by a sweeping desire for freedom; once forgotten, and swept under the rug.

"My days have passed, my plans are shattered. Yet the desires of my heart turn night into day; in the face of the darkness light is near" (Job 17: 11-12)

Secrets of a small town girl now grown to woman, living under the shadow of death, are revealed through the eyes of an innocent wife of youth. When everything in my life unraveled, God's perseverance provided a way of escape, and just in the nick of time.

"...on those living in the land of the shadow of death a light has dawned" (Matthew 4:16)

"Do not be deceived: God cannot be mocked. A man reaps what he sows" (Galatians 6:7)

—J. HANNAH LLOYD

"Even though I walk through the darkest valley, I will fear no evil, for you are with me..." (Psalms 23:4)

Foreword

By

Ann Tatlock

The first time I met J. Hannah Lloyd, she was smiling. We were both attending a women's Bible study at the Billy Graham Training Center at the Cove when we happened to end up—providentially, I'm sure—in the same small group. Over the next several weeks, I became acquainted with a sweet, serene, God-loving woman who seemed perfectly at peace with herself, and the world.

Nothing about her hinted at what none of us could see—the long history of unthinkable abuse that lay in her past. Only months later, after our friendship deepened, did she share with me her story of verbal and physical abuse at the hands of her pastor-husband.

I was stunned to realize both the atmosphere of rage in which she was forced to live for years, as well as the physical violence that resulted in black eyes, bruises and broken bones. The abuse eventually escalated to include death threats and yet, broken and afraid, she resigned to her fate. She tried to live the outward life of a pastor's wife and mother of three young children while hiding from everyone around her the truth of what she faced daily at home.

Perhaps one of the most heartbreaking parts of her story is that when she finally did begin to seek help, no one believed her. Not her family. Not her in-laws. Not even law enforcement. How could a man who was a pastor be abusing his wife?

Sadly, the author's narrative of domestic violence is

hardly an isolated event. An estimated one in every three women worldwide will experience gender-based violence during their lifetime. Multitudes of women are abused daily—yes, even in Christian homes.

Changed hearts and the healing of marriages is the ideal. But in our broken world, that doesn't always happen. And when it doesn't happen, there comes a time when escape is imperative. After years of adhering to the erroneous idea that divorce is an unforgiveable sin, Hannah realized her only hope of survival was to escape. Such escape takes considerable courage and an unshakable faith in God. She had both.

As she clung to the Lord for help, she discovered everything she needed to escape and survive was provided by his hand. He led her to a new place, one of healing and joy. And ultimately, he blessed her with a new marriage based on love and respect. Hannah's story is perhaps one of the greatest testimonies to God's grace I have ever known.

Maybe you are where Hannah once was, or perhaps you know someone else who is caught up in an abusive relationship. When you read this story you will know one thing for sure: There is hope. God not only can help you, he *will* help you. He *desires* to help you. You can discover, as she did, that the God who made us is also the God who is able to make all things new.

—ANN TATLOCK
2012 Christy Award Winner
Named by Booklist Magazine as one of the
Top Ten Historical Novelists of the year
Award-winning Author, Teacher,
Conference speaker

Introduction

Tied to Terror

My escape from mistreatment, cruelty, and violence would happen. Of this I was certain, or I would die trying.

"...you are a shield around me, O LORD; you bestow glory on me and lift up my head. In You, O LORD, I put my trust. Let me never be put to shame" (Psalms 3: 3, 71:1)

Twelve years of an aggressive marriage had been a vicious journey. But following a final sadistic assault that caused serious bodily injury, my battle to survive was more than critical. Rigid authority and strict discipline received as a child permitted tolerance, but never retaliation while married. Instead I must seek an alternative resolution in order to survive.

Horrendous scars of malicious brutality, shame, and abuse inflicted by a violent husband's embrace had, over time, crushed all hope for a happy and productive existence—or so I believed.

Guidance from above, coupled with a desire to live, then produced enough motivation to shape a secret plan of escape from my abuser. A restraining order and separation agreement in hand, I plunged headlong into the future with nothing but faith in the God of my salvation. My status was now posted as single mom, with three small children in tow.

"Look upon my suffering and deliver me, for I have not forgotten your law. Defend my cause and redeem me; preserve my life according to your promise. Direct my footsteps according to your word; let no sin rule over me. Redeem me from the oppression of men, that I may obey your precepts" (Psalms 119:153-154, 133-134)

Two concerned colleagues, realizing the conditions of my marriage were life-threatening, provided needed assistance in returning to the home of my parents. Money was tight, almost non-existent. But a reprieve from violence on a daily basis was remarkable. One miracle then followed another as I learned to rely on God for my very existence.

His promises are true, and have been proven again and again throughout the years. My escape from abuse is a testimony of God's grace, and a restoration of joy my reward. With complete abandonment, and absolute faith in God, I can now live each day to the fullest—no strings attached.

Chapter One

Keeper of the Peace

The rain pounded in waves and torrents as Hannah closed the door behind her husband. "I'm glad he's gone," she whispered, and breathed a quick prayer of thanksgiving. Still her body quivered, so she took a deep breath. She slowly released, then walked to her desk, and reached for her journal. But tears shed the night before had drenched the book, and the pages were sticking together.

Anger, hurt, and remorse over the harshness of her reality again ignited, allowing un-restrained tears to flood her heart, and again drench the journal. Her brow then furrowed, her writing pen repositioned, and she again surrendered the truth of her existence to the crumpled pages of a secret diary.

When Jeremy and I first married, we were happy. At least I thought we were. But the puzzle of a stable marriage has never quite fallen into place. The rigors of maintaining a calm environment now keeps me anxious, stressed out, and frazzled to the max.

When angry, Jeremy's violence conveys a serious lack of self-control. His overbearing dominance then keeps me busy making amends for everything wrong in his life. Our marriage is now a complete disaster. But, my prayer *was* answered. He did marry me. Is it now my fault our marriage was on the rocks shortly after it began?

I feel trapped, paralyzed, and afraid. Other times I'm proud of my pastor-husband. His message of deliverance rings out as true. Everyone loves him, and believes he's wonderful. People even pray through to salvation under his ministry. And, he *is* good looking.

His ability to minister is astounding. But his inability to appreciate me, his wife, is heartbreaking. Hiding evidence to maintain the peace is now an everyday affair. Yet those around me seem unaware of my problems.

Assaults at home are crushing, painful, and intimidating. Jeremy's actions simply didn't make sense. But clues of his character reveal he will do whatever's necessary to make himself appear as one who cares. In the aftermath, this keeps me a prisoner of fear and abuse. I want to run away. I want escape. But can I? Who can I trust?

Voices in my head scream isolation, despair, and hopelessness—even hell and divorce. Fire blazes through my ankles even though I'm not yet divorced. I know how the church feels, and how my family will react if we separate. But, my life is nothing more than a lie. *What if divorce lands me in the bad place?*

An embedded image of romance past then softened her heart, and she recalled moments when the word defeat could only be found in a dictionary. But after a tedious sigh, she closed the journal, gazed far into the distance, and recalled the way it all began.

A short week-end visit with a friend had landed them both in church on Sunday. But a handsome man sitting across the aisle caught her eye, and then snagged her heart. His handsome charm kept her glancing in his direction. On the inside her heart pounded restlessly.

"—who is that?" she asked, aiming her finger at the man who had claimed her attention all morning.

Olivia smiled, and then winked back. "That's Jeremy, the man I was telling you about," she said. "He's an evangelist, and a pretty good preacher."

"Can you introduce us?"

She hesitated, and then complied. "Jeremy, this is my friend—Hannah, this is Jeremy."

"H—Hi Jeremy," Hannah said, but then her face flamed, and she quickly turned away.

"Hello back to you," he said, followed by laugh. His words, smooth and mellow, dissolved her heart; and she melted beneath his gaze.

Then, in calm response, he reached out his hand, grasped hers, and slowly released. And so began her new life—the one she had dreamed about her entire life.

Chapter Two

Jitters

"Let's get married."

"Let's elope."

"I asked first."

"Let's keep this a secret, "Hannah said. "I'm not even telling Olivia until the marriage certificate is in my hand." And, with those words, the decision was sealed. The following Monday, the day after Easter, was the planned day.

Early that morning, as the fragrance of spring surrounded them, Hannah and Jeremy sped to the courthouse. Their required documentation was in hand, ready to succor their marriage vows. The judge, an elderly gentleman with a receding hairline, imparted words of wisdom after pronouncing them as married. "Remember and put God first in everything you do," he said, and then placed the marriage certificate in Jeremy's hands.

At that moment all that mattered was young love, yet held no true promise of happiness. Little did Hannah know her dream would soon begin to un-ravel. And just days into the marriage, torrential downpours of anger dumped on her for any and all infractions began to hold her hostage. But she was in this marriage for the duration. Her commitment was solid, and firmly grounded. God would be her anchor; or so she believed. And so she brushed aside her fears, and tried to forget her concerns.

***

After work one afternoon, Jeremy pulled his jacket close and stepped back outside. In response Hannah pulled her own wrap on, and followed close behind; shoes clicking and clacking on the uneven pavement in rhythmic accents.

"How long will you be gone?" she asked as the door to his outdated Toyota closed.

"Oh, probably a couple of hours," he said, and then shot his famous smile back. "I'll be back before you know it. The pastor's meeting shouldn't last too long."

"I'll miss you."

"I'll miss you too, baby."

She smiled, stepped from the curb, and then mouthed, "See you soon," before jiggling her hand in slow motion.

"Come here a minute," he said, then stepped back out of the car. "How about a kiss for the road?"

Leaning over, she quickly melted into his open arms. But as hot lips met, her mind began to drift. The next instant he pulled away.

"I really need to go," he said, "or I'll be late." Then, without another word, he jumped in his car, waved, and drove away.

Hannah's heart splintered as she gazed after him. But once the car rolled out of sight, she trudged back to their tiny bungalow, and closed the door. Still she was glad they were tight. Being Jeremy's wife was accelerating, and she relished every moment spent with him. Although sharing him with the church was inevitable, that was something she was willing to do.

***

Again glancing at the clock, she let out a long sign. Where was Jeremy?

The next instant a grinding noise from the outside caught her attention, and she jumped in quick response. Tires were spinning up the driveway. The car then stopped, and Jeremy ran up the porch steps into the house.

"Hi, Jeremy—you're finally home" she said, reaching out. But in response, he pushed her aside, threw his keys on a table, and strode to the kitchen.

"You don't need to worry about me," he said. His words were acid.

"I'm just glad you're home," she said, hands still outstretched. But again he turned away.

"I'm hungry," he said, then jerked the refrigerator open. "What's for dinner?"

"I made a casserole," she said. "It's cold, but I can heat it up." *Why didn't he kiss me?*

"I don't like casseroles," he said, but sounded agitated. "What's in it?"

"Pasta and chicken," she said, proud of her accomplishment. "It's good—Mother's recipe."

"Never mind," he said, and a frown formed. "I'm going to Mom's and get some real food."

"What's wrong?" she asked, somewhat startled. "I cooked this especially for you."

"I'm not in the mood," he said. "Now stay out of my way."

Never before had Jeremy acted this way. Why was he mad?

"Just leave me alone," he said. "Where are my keys?"

"Don't leave. What happened at the meeting?"

"Nothing you need to know about," he snapped.

His words, still sour, were troubling; and Hannah stepped aside. But instead of apologizing, he turned, shuffled through some papers on the table, and then strode to the door.

"Please," she said, again reaching out. But his eyes glazed, and, with a hand of steel, struck her across the face. Her back then slammed the table, causing it to slide hard from the impact. The next instant her cheek flamed, and tender tears formed.

"What did I do? What did I do wrong?"

"Leave me alone, bitch," he hissed. "Just leave me alone."

She was stunned.

But after rebalancing, she rubbed her reddened cheek; and brushed away hot tears. "I don't understand," she said, crushed. A second punch then landed, and this time her body fell backward into a kitchen cabinet.

"I'm leaving now," he said; face, clinched and unreadable. He then turned, and stomped to the door.

Confused and still rubbing her jaw, Hannah pulled herself up and ran after him. "What did I do? Why did you hit me?" she asked.

But he only glared back, jumped in his car, and then sped away.

Understanding was impossible. But should she keep his actions a secret? He was, after all, a good preacher. Besides, she wasn't ready to wreck his reputation. Maybe, she told herself, maybe she just needed more time to learn how to be a better wife. He could change—with her help. It was important—for the sake of the ministry. Besides, his childhood had probably difficult without a father in the home.

Confidence in herself then filled her heart. "Mother always told me being punished would make me stronger," she whispered. Maybe I needed to be punched. The Bible says a wife is her husband's helper. That means I'm Jeremy's helper."

Although shattered in body and perplexed in mind, she lifted her hands upward, then reached for her Bible; searching for words of consultation. Then, as her eye rested on the third Book of Philippians, verse thirteen, she resigned herself to forgiveness.

"Brothers, I do not consider myself yet to have taken hold of it. But one thing I do: Forgetting what is behind and straining toward what is ahead, I press on toward the goal to win the prize for which God has called me heavenward in Christ Jesus"

Chapter Three

Puzzle Pieces

The following morning Jeremy was his old self again. After apologies, hugs, and kisses, his pleas of forgiveness were accepted. And yet Hannah was apprehensive, and unable to understand his rage. But she swallowed her pride—just happy things were back on track. Their planned trip to Hendersonville would be fun. She would make sure of that. He needed to meet her parents, and they needed to meet him.

***

Her father, as a welcoming gesture, displayed a collection of guns and rifles for his new son-in-law to examine. But Jeremy's interest in one particular piece was motivation enough to give them the rifle 'for safe keeping.'

"Let's buy some bullets," Jeremy said on the way home. "I want to try this baby out, and see how good it shoots."

Yet, for some unknown reason, panic seized Hannah's mind. Funny she'd never before noticed how high strung, self-centered, and flamboyant he was. Still, for now, staying one step ahead of the game would be safest.

Once home, he was all about the gun.

"Let's put some cans on this old stump," he said after aiming at trees for several minutes. "They will make good targets."

Several empty cans were then placed in neat rows on

the stump, and Hannah stepped back to watch.

"Is that the best you can do?" she asked, and tried to squelch a laugh. "You've missed half the cans, and the others are falling over."

"Shut up—shut up," he said, then moved his shoulders in circles as if to loosen them. He then reloaded the gun, and aimed again.

"I'll knock them all off this time," he said, the pitch in his voice rising. "Just watch and see." His face then reddened, and hers tensed.

"What if he turns the gun on me?" she whispered.

But she shook off her apprehension, and concentrated on the action at hand. She was, after all, in love. "And love covers a multitude of sins, right?"

***

More odd actions were beginning to surface, and Hannah couldn't understand why. What was happening to her marriage? And why was Jeremy pulling away from her? Did he regret getting married? In her heart she was beginning to think he did. And yet they both believed marriage was forever.

While dating they often talked about God's guidance in their lives. How God wanted him to preach. But dreams of speaking to large crowds while leading many to salvation were foremost in his mind.

In the past he prayed all the time. Now he rarely spoke a blessing over their food. "Why, God? Why?"

Chapter Four

Christmas Gift

Their first Christmas as newlyweds needed to be special, if only a single box of ornaments and a few lights were in the budget. Christmas was Hannah's favorite time of year.

Several days before the holiday, and after Jeremy left for work, she pulled her sweater close. Winter was in full swing. Blustery wind whistled through tiny holes and unsealed crevices in the outside wall. On the inside, the bungalow's window panes and shallow frames creaked and squeaked from the bluster.

But as the squall continued, she scurried about; decorating their home for the upcoming season. And, in a short amount of time, a newly decorated tree sported colorful lights and assorted baubles ready for Jeremy's return home.

"I'm so excited," she whispered as shivers of excitement ran up and down her spine. She could hardly wait for the big day.

Early Christmas morning, as soon as daybreak flickered through the window panes, they both climbed out of bed, and meandered to the tree. One gift, lovingly swathed in reds and greens, was then handed to Jeremy.

"Hurry up and open this one," she said, words slurring in the excitement of the moment.

Jeremy grinned, reached for the gift, and then ripped through the paper as he reached to comply. The next instant a metal container full of assorted hand tools and accessories jetted across the room, and slammed their newly purchased furniture. The tools spilled, and then spread in colorful array across the floor. Chipped fragments of wooden debris from the headboard and bureau also littered the floor.

"Who do you think I am—a handyman?" he asked, eyes full of fire. "I'm a preacher, remember?"

Tears began to stream down Hannah's cheeks as she bolted to retrieve the gift. The tools were then gathered and again placed in the container. But when she glanced up, still holding the case, Jeremy's face was turnip red.

"I thought you'd like my present," she said, meek and apologetic. "You didn't have any."

His glare only made her shiver. "I—I'm sorry," she said. What else could she say?

Still glowering, he turned and stomped from the room. Enraged words of profanity and rage, spoke in anger, filtered back to her ears.

She had been isolated most of her life, and wasn't accustomed to cursing, or vulgarity. Neither had she observed course actions while growing up. In fact, she had never been treated this way, and instantly felt isolated, and rejected. This was unchartered territory, and she wasn't sure how to react, or what to do.

"I'll have to do better," she promised herself. "After all, keeping my husband happy is my responsibility."

***

An abrupt blast from the outside suddenly rattled their sleep, causing Hannah to bolt upright. Seconds later more explosions echoed through the neighborhood.

"Oh, no," she said, clutching her head. "I forgot all about New Year's."

"Get the rifle," Jeremy said, grabbing his pants and coat. "I'm going to make some real noise."

But while waiting for him to dress, she stared outside through the closed window; and watched for bright flashes of firework residue. At the same time she wondered if he should even shoot the gun. Did she dare speak her thoughts?

"Bullets aren't fireworks, you know," she said. Her words, although brave, were spoken with caution.

"Who cares?" he asked; then jerked the rifle from the rack, turned on his heel, and headed out the door.

"Please, come back inside," she said as gusts of frigid air flooded the inside through the opened door. "You might get in trouble." But when a shot ripped through the air, she decided to join him on the dimly lit porch. Once outside, she pulled her robe even tighter.

"You really shouldn't shoot that gun," she said.

The next instant an outside light illuminated, and a door across the street opened. A robust man, shaking his fist, then stepped through the opening. "What do you think you're doing?" he yelled, looking in their direction. He turned, strode to the corner of his home, and began examining the façade. Jeremy, on the other hand, looked dazed.

"You'd better go talk to him," Hannah said, urging him forward.

"Guess I can't hide from this one," he said, glancing around. "Guess I'll go see what I hit."

Still the neighbor's manifested anger continued, so she said a quick prayer, and then watched in silence. But when Jeremy reached the man, they began to closely examine the house. Minutes later Jeremy gaited back across the street, a grin on his face.

"The man said it's alright," he said, panting. "Only nicked the corner. Told me not to shoot his house again, or I'd be in real trouble."

Hannah touched him gently on the arm. "I'm just glad he's not mad," she said.

"He said if I did it again, he would call the police."

She let out a long sigh, then held the door open for Jeremy, who slid inside.

"That was a close call," he said, then flopped on a chair, glanced at her, and howled with laughter.

Chapter Five

Slammed

Jeremy's fist came fast and hard, and Hannah's nose went instantly numb. *Why did he hit me? Why is he so angry? What did I do?*

"Please help me, God," she whispered. Her hands, now shaking, were gripped in fear.

The next instant he began rummaging through the bureau drawer. He glanced up, shot her a look of contempt, and then removed several of her childhood keepsakes; all the while snickering in a mocking way.

Dismayed, she watched in horror as he strode to the oil circulator, grabbed a cloth to cover the handle, and jerked the lid open. Still laughing, he tossed two figurines of Bach and Beethoven into the fire.

"Please stop. Please don't—" she said. And, in desperation, wrung her hands. "Those are my trophies—from piano recital. I earned them."

But he ignored her pleas, and, instead, reached for their newly processed pictures. He ripped them all in half, glanced at her, and then tossed the entire packet in the fire. But his eyes were fiery, and she cowered beneath his gaze. Still she needed to stop him before he destroyed anything else.

"Stop, please—," she said, brave but frightened.

"Shut up. Shut up, you ugly bitch," he said. More harsh profanity then rolled from his lips in words she had never before heard from him. The next instant a fist slammed her face, her jaw popped, and she instantly felt the tightening of swelling flesh.

Will he ever stop hitting me? And why is he so mad? Maybe it's because I was a late getting home from the store. He might be jealous, or something. But why?

Circulated rumors of women beaten by husbands were rare in Hannah's small world. Although she recalled many punishments as a child, never one of being hit with a fist. Well, her father's back-handed slaps were unforgettable, as were the many whelps that covered her arms and legs throughout childhood. But Jeremy shouldn't get angry. He was a preacher.

Maybe he needs to vent. I guess it's okay for him to hit me. After all, I am his wife. But what I did I do that was so terrible?

All night long course words and tempered battering held her captive. But when daylight emerged, tears no longer fell from her eyes. Having surrendered to exhaustion and pummels, she was drained, emotionless, and withdrawn.

She dragged herself to a chair; curled up, and closed her eyes. But she opened them again at the sound of sopping.

"I'm sorry," Jeremy said again and again. "Please forgive me. You know I love you." He slid down beside the chair, knelt, and then stroked her face.

Hannah, eyes now open, only stared at him.

"I really am sorry I hit you," he said again, and his arm drew her close. "I didn't mean to hit you. I was mad. You know I love you."

But the urge to resist was strong. Her nose was bleeding. Her lips were split. And, her spirit was sagging. She was more than bruised. She was confused. What about all the things he had just destroyed? She couldn't replace any one of them. What about her bruises? What about the rip in her heart?

Still, she wanted her marriage to work. And because she was also embarrassed, keeping her mouth shut was essential—because the word defeat did not yet exist in her mind.

"I love you, too," she said—words spoken, but not felt. And, to keep the peace, a hug of forgiveness given, although forced.

"Are you okay?" a church member asked as, together, she and Jeremy climbed the church steps later that same morning.

"I—I think so," she said. But her words were automatic, and she rubbed her tongue over a chipped tooth.

"Please, God, don't let anyone else notice," she whispered. "I don't want them feeling sorry for me."

They didn't.

***

Would life always be this way? All Hannah ever wanted was someone to truly love her. But now, trapped without the possibility of escaping her destiny, her existence was more than confusing. Childhood discipline and church training had long before indoctrinated her convictions. She was stuck.

Her parents would disown her if she divorced. The church would turn her out if she left Jeremy. And, for some odd reason, all her close friends had suddenly disappeared. Already signs of the battered wife syndrome were visible, yet ignored by those around her.

Then taking note of skeptic reactions, she realized disbelief was inevitable; and decided to simply keep Jeremy's actions to herself. Embarrassment over the battering, fear of rejection, and apprehension of probable doubt allowed a decision of silence.

***

Three years into the marriage and a pattern of abuse was in place. Episodes of battering would begin with slaps to the face, and cumulate into kicks, and fist-impressions on head and arm. It wasn't every day, but frequent enough to be bothersome.

Jeremy, now the pastor of a church some distance away, but within driving distance, held an irreproachable and prominent stance. It was important, for the sake of the church and his family, that Hannah applaud and respect him as others did.

Although the church was tiny, this intermit was the building blocks to Jeremy's future. Yet she was only a shadow of his increasing popularity and growing status among the congregants. Her contributions were in the music department, but often devalued, and perceived less important than his. And, she knew her place.

***

Late one Sunday evening, after returning home, Jeremy stood in front of her, and gritted his teeth. "Why did you stay and talk to Sister Rogers after church?" he asked.

All Hannah could do was shrug her shoulders.

"You knew I wanted to go straight home and watch the game on TV."

This conversation wasn't going well, so she laid her purse on a chair, turned and faced him. "I forgot," was all she could say. "I simply forgot."

The next instant a fist rammed her face, and her legs instantly gave way. The force of impact then landed her on the floor, where another blow caught her on the shoulder.

"You never listen, do you?" he asked.

But she refused to answer. Instead, she pulled herself up. Yet before she could again move, clammy hands were propelling her down the hallway.

It was futile staying balanced, and she stumbled forward; tripping over her own two feet as she plunged headlong into the abyss. Jeremy's breath, hot on her neck, made her quiver; and she inhaled in staggering gulps of air.

"Please stop. Please," she begged, shoulders mush beneath his strength.

"Stay out of my way," he said, and formed a nubby fist for another round. "Get up."

Again lunging forward, he shoved a harden fist into her head. "Get up, you mother-fucking whore," he said. His words were cold, and she was instantly scared of her wits. How could he be a preacher, and beat his wife? How could he stand in front of church people and preach? And how could he give an alter call, and people come?

Terrified, she wrapped her arms around the top of her head as another blow knocked her backward. But as she looked around from her spot on the floor, she realized there was no way to escape—no way out. The door to the outside was at the far end of the hall.

Still shaken, she glanced down at blood droplets spattering the top of her folded legs; and new terror gripped her by the throat.

"You stupid bitch," he said. More vulgarity and degrading words followed. But his words, spoken through gritted teeth, challenged, and were full of hate.

She pushed herself into a standing position, reached inside the bathroom, and grabbed a towel bar for support. The next instant she was sprawled over the bathtub. Now winded, and gasping for air, she tried get up, but the cold porcelain held her hostage.

"You ugly bitch," he said, voice course and unrelenting. But as more degrading words erupted, she withdrew farther into herself, closed her eyes, and lifted up a silent prayer for guidance.

"I'll blow your fucking brains out, you ugly whore," he said.

She cowered beneath his gaze. But could she survive another terrorizing onslaught?

"I promise I'll kill you. And, it will be soon."

Again he lunged, and his eyes blazed. "Now get up bitch."

His boot then kicked her sharply in the thigh, and she slumped forward. The sting of harsh slaps, and the throb of aching bones, now held her at his command. The next instant his boot met another intended target, and bashed her upper thigh with blunt force. The heaviness of hardened leather then crushed her leg as it twisted around her lower extremities.

"Oh, God—help me. Please help me. Please don't let him hit me again. Please—"

Again his fist rammed her shoulder. But she sucked in the pain, and refused to verbally surrender. Although words of urgency were released, they were silent. "Oh, God—help me!"

"If you ever try to leave me, I swear, I'll blow your fucking brains out," he said. His rage was ballistic.

"He's going to kill me," she whispered.

"You have nowhere to go," he said, laughing. "Besides, you'll never make it on your own."

Again his boot landed on her thigh, as added emphasis. He then turned, and, without another word, slunk from the room; leaving her to suffer on her own.

"Please God—help me. It hurts," she said, still struggling against the tub. Her body, now drenched with sweat, throbbed and ached with each labored breath. But once on her feet, she limped to the side, grabbed a hand mirror, and grimaced. A swollen face and purple eye stared back at her

With an index finger, she traced an uneven path down her cheek where blood and tears formed a trail to her breast. *I can't live like this. I simply can't do it anymore. I need help.*

Still balancing, she slid her torso along the wall to the bedroom, and staggered to the bed. She then eased down on the mattress, and let go; sinking deep into the cool, unruffled spread. Lesions and newly formed bruises were now throbbing incessantly.

"Oh God, what is my purpose?" she cried out. "I'm the wife of a preacher who enjoys seeing me in pain."

Nothing seemed to please Jeremy, no matter what she did. It was time to talk to the police, or someone in authority. The church and her parents would be no help. She also had serious doubt about his family, although one of his sisters had recently noticed some injuries, and questioned the reason. Perhaps she had an advocate after all.

"Oh, God, how did I ever get in this mess?" she said out loud.

Chapter Six

Jail Bird

Although stiff and sore, Monday again found Hannah at work as Office Manager of a local radio station. But as the day progressed, she mulled over what to do; and decided to tell Ashley, one of Jeremy's sisters, of her brother's actions—looking for direction and sympathy.

Later, after work, and barely able to walk upright, she somehow managed to stagger inside the department store where Ashley was straightening perfumes behind a mirrored counter. Then, after a ragged breath, she tapped the surface to get her attention.

"I turned Jeremy in at the sheriff's department," she said, and released a long sigh.

In an instant Ashley turned, and looked her in the eye. "Did you really?" she asked, a shocked look on her face.

"He knocked me over the bathtub and cussed me out last night. The last time you and I talked, you said I should turn him in to the police if he assaulted me again."

"Yes, I know I did," Ashley said, looking somber. "I just didn't think you'd do it." Then she turned away, and swiped a duster along the edge of the shelving.

"I didn't know what else to do," Hannah said, then leaned forward; resting her arms on the counter top. "You said that was the only way to stop him from hitting me. I thought you'd be happy I finally did something."

"Well, Jeremy is my brother, you know," Ashley said, again straightening bottles. "Maybe you did the right thing. Maybe you didn't."

"Please don't be mad," Hannah said, and her lips drew into a thin line. "I thought you knew I'd do it."

"When is he getting arrested?"

"Today—after he gets off work," Hannah said. But then her stomach tensed, and bundled nerves began to tie her flesh in knots. "I'm really not happy about any of this."

"When did you sign the warrant?"

"Today. I went to see a magistrate today."

"Well, you knew he would get arrested, didn't you?"

"Not at first. I only wanted to see what her options were."

Hannah's heart was now pounding, and she shifted into another position; trying to understand Ashley's reaction. But Ashley only turned and walked to a phone behind the counter.

"Does anybody in church know besides me?" she asked.

"I don't know. How would they?"

"Does Mom know?"

"No."

"I'm calling her now," she said, and lifted the phone.

"What will the church do if they find out?" Hannah whispered to herself. "Besides, my in-laws are closer than my own family. I certainly don't want to hurt them."

Beads of sweat began to pop out on her forehead, and she reached up to wipe them away. *Why did I talk to that magistrate? Maybe I should've left things alone and not said anything. What if Jeremy beats me up again for having him arrested?*

A customer then walked past, and Hannah stepped aside. The next instant her legs wobbled and she grabbed the counter for support. Her lips were now dry, and she moistened them with the tip of her tongue. *Did I do the right thing? Well, maybe not. But, Jeremy's been hitting me with his fist. He said I deserved it. Maybe I did. But no—I don't deserve being hit that way. I'm not a kid anymore. I'm an adult. Adults don't need that type of correction.*

Later that evening, after returning home, Hannah heard a small knock at the door. Mrs. Allen, Jeremy's mother, was standing outside.

Suddenly weak, she took a deep breath, and then opened the door. Mrs. Allen smiled a half-smile, glanced behind her, and then stepped inside. Jeremy, looking anxious, followed close behind. But after the door closed, Hannah dropped down on an ottoman, eyes wide.

"How did you get out of jail?" she asked, looking directly at Jeremy. But then she lowered her head. "Well, I guess I know," she said softly. And a large sigh escaped.

"Why don't you two make up?" Mrs. Allen asked.

"I'm sorry I hit you," he said, and huge tears filled his eyes. "I promise. I'll never do it again."

It was obvious he had been coached. His crocodile tears looked staged. But then Hannah caught his eye. "You still have to go to court," she said.

"You can drop the charges, can't you?" He was now begging.

"I don't know if I should."

"Please." And he fell to his knees. "I promise I'll never hit you again."

"I'll think about it."

He is, after all, a preacher. I have to trust him, don't I? His reputation will be shot if I don't drop the charges. How could anyone survive a scandal like that? Thankfully, the church is miles away from where we live. They'll never know anything happened.

"I guess I'll drop them," she told herself. Everybody wants me to."

Three months later she was pregnant with their first child.

Chapter Seven

Stones to Throw

Thank God the doctor's office is only one block away. An overwhelming concentration of pain shrouded Hannah's stance as she hoisted ten-month-old Haley to her side. Still in pain, she walked the short trek as fast as her legs would allow. A few minutes later she was inside the building.

In the waiting room she dropped her purse on a bench, and gingerly positioned herself after sitting the baby down. She then grabbed her back. The pain was excruciating.

Now agitated, she lifted her purse, and searched deep inside. But once the aspirin bottle was located, she swallowed the remaining tablets. *Where is that doctor? And why is he so slow?*

At last her name was called, and she dragged herself to the examining room.

"You look like you're in pain," the nurse said.

"It's killing me," Hannah said, again rubbing her back. "It's worse than labor pain."

"I'll get the doctor right now, no more waiting," the nurse said; then turned, and reached for Haley. "I'll take the baby with me, and leave her up front with the receptionist, if you like."

"Yes, thanks," Hannah said, grateful the baby would be safe. Lamaze breaths and controlled breathing then helped control the pain, but the technique only reinforced an urgency to fight her way beyond whatever was causing the anguish.

It was pointless calling Jeremy. She knew he wouldn't care if she felt alone, and helpless.

Minutes later, after a urine test and several excruciating positions on an x-ray table, Hannah was more than ready for the doctor's analysis. In fact, she was anxious to get up and go about her day; if only the torture would stop.

"I'm giving you're an injection for the pain," Dr. Capps said. "You'll feel better after the medication takes effect.

***

Later, as she rested, the throbbing ceased. But then she was dizzy—and giddy. Blinking to stay awake was barely working, and she struggled to keep her eyes open. "Should I let myself go to sleep?" she whispered. "What about Haley?"

"You have kidney stones," the doctor said, when he returned. She could only stare at him.

"I've called the hospital. Looks like the stones are too large to pass," he said, and patted her on the shoulder. "They're waiting for you in Emergency."

"Where's my baby?" she asked, but sounded as if encased in a jar.

"Up front with the receptionist," the nurse said. "We need to call someone to take you to the hospital."

"My husband's at work," Hannah said, but her words slurred. "My, uh, sister-in-law."

"Do you have a number?"

Several digits were then recited. And, in what seemed like seconds, Ashley was standing beside her in the room.

"I'll take Haley home with me after I take you to the hospital," she said.

At least the baby would be in good hands. At this point Hannah doubted Jeremy would care either way.

***

Fourteen days in the hospital was taking its toll. Depression was taking its toll—so much so the staff psychologist was now visiting Hannah on a regular basis. Stitches and scar tissue now covered half the expanse of her body. And, she was more alone and isolated than ever before.

"I miss her baby," she said, words whispered every night as tears fell like rain. Already Haley first steps were history. What else had she missed?

"You're going home today," the nurse said as she straightened the pillow beneath Hannah's head. She smiled, then slipped a fresh straw into a Styrofoam cup on the tray.

"I am?" Hannah asked. And the beginnings of a grin shaped her lips. "Are you sure?"

"The doctor will be in shortly to release you," the nurse said, still smiling. "Go ahead and make arrangements to be picked up. Today's your day."

At last she was going home, and her heart raced with anticipation. She could hardly wait to hold her again.

"I'm taking the week off," Jeremy said as he rolled the squeaky wheel chair down a long hospital corridor. Hannah's lap, piled high with flowers, magazines, and a small suitcase, was filled to capacity. The response to her hospitalization from family and church had been overwhelming.

"I'll be able to change your bandages when you need them changed," he said.

The chair then came to an abrupt halt, giving Hannah a chance to reinforce her thoughts. But she chose her words carefully. "Remember what the doctor said." And, as a distraction, she straightened a magazine ready to slide off her lap. "My bandage needs changing several times a day. He said the incision will drain about one week."

"I'll be around," Jeremy said, and the chair was again on the roll. "Don't worry about a thing."

Although she reserved some doubt, at least she was going home.

***

Poor Haley. She hardly knew who Hannah was. As for Jeremy, his actions hadn't changed at all. His promise to provide assistance were only words. And, as the week progressed, so did Hannah's workload; and his outings. They were as detailed as a power map. But rude comments about surgical scars she could do without.

Reaching around her back, she again taped another bandage into place. At least the tubes were producing less and less.

Jeremy's family believed he was helping her. And so did the church. But, again, Jeremy was fooling everyone.

She dropped another soiled bandage into the trash, and again released her anguish. Changing bandages was hard. Another pain pill and she edged toward the bathroom. It was time to gather more soiled laundry. If she didn't keep the clothes clean, who would?

Grunting for energy and momentum, she shoved a ton of dirty laundry into the washing machine, and turned the dial. Meanwhile, Haley was crying for attention.

"Oh, God. Please help me through this day," she said out loud. But her words were strained as, once again, she inched along the wall. *Where was Jeremy? I wonder—did he take golf clubs or a tennis racket this time?*

Chapter Eight

The Appointment

Six hours of labor through the night produced an eight pound-five-ounce boy with auburn hair and blue eyes. Austin's arrival early Wednesday morning brought new joy to Hannah's shattered heart. But as she cuddled the new baby in her arms, Jeremy stepped in the room.

"Look what came in the mail," he said, and a huge smile covered his face. He then waved a large manila envelope. The return address read Superintendent of the Holiness Conference.

"I've been accepted as pastor of a church just across the state line," he said. "My second pastorate."

"Well, I guess today calls for a double celebration," Hannah said, and forced a smile.

"I can't wait," he said, then reached for the baby; holding him for the first time since his birth hours earlier. "I'm riding up this afternoon to check out the church building."

"Are you coming by to see us again?"

"I'll swing by tomorrow," he said, then handed the baby back. "I'm doing some visitation too."

"Guess what happened after you left this morning?"

"What?"

"The nurse gave Austin his first bath in front of all the new moms," she said. "He was the demonstration baby on how to bathe an infant. I was so proud of him, even though he didn't like the bath very much."

"That's funny," he said. "But listen. I found out the

church is really excited we're coming."

But Hannah was more focused on the new baby than a new church assignment.

"They're giving us a baby shower next week," he said.

"Nice," she said, followed by a frown. Then she slid up higher in bed. "I get out of the hospital Friday."

"I won't forget," he said.

Later, as he fingered through a magazine, she dozed. But when he bumped the tray table, her eyes popped open.

"I need to go," he said, and dropped the magazine on a table.

"How's Haley?" she asked, as memories of bright blue eyes glimmered in her head.

"I think she misses you. At least that's what Ashley said."

"I hope she doesn't forget who I am again."

"Okay," he said, and again glanced at his watch. "I need to run. I have a funeral to perform this afternoon before I go and see the new church."

Later, after he left, the baby was breastfed, and fell asleep in Hannah's arms. Still, having babies was easy compared to life at home. Two babies and a new church assignment would certainly keep this pastor's wife busy.

***

"You'll never be any help to me as a pastor's wife," Jeremy said as they headed to the new church several weeks later.

His words stung. Why was he so critical? Not only was Hannah the church pianist—required attendance—but wasn't her role as his wife also relevant?

Piles of sheet music and printed verse were kept ready, as well as ideas for the choir. Preparing lessons for children's church was also important. Even her janitorial skills were crucial. She couldn't justify his words. What exactly did he mean? But instead of responding, she stared through the car window, and remained silent.

"You're not wearing that ugly thing again, are you?" he asked. "You don't even know how to dress. Plus, you're fat now."

Jeremy's words again wrenched her heart. *Why does he say such mean things to me? Recovery from childbirth is still ongoing.*

"You don't even know what to say to people," he said. "I have to tell you what to say, you're so stupid." His laughter then whipped through the air. "You look like an old hag—you old hag."

He used to love me—told me I was beautiful. We used to be crazy about each other. Two kids later and I'm an old hag? What happened?

Looking down she couldn't help but note the out-of-style dress she wore that came to her knees. She didn't own pretty clothes. Extra money always bought updates for his wardrobe.

Neck ties of various color and design now decorated the bedroom door. Suits of modern style and cut filled the closet. Crisp white shirts, pressed and separately hung remained clean, neat, and ready to wear. Dress shoes, both brown and black, finished the collection; and were kept polished and fresh. Her job was simply making sure his clothing was immaculate.

Church doctrine required that women wear only dresses, as pants, and heaven forbid, shorts and swimwear, were banned as sinful. Make-up and jewelry, even the wedding band, was out of the question. Clothing for women was simple, and basic. No frills to enhance their attire. But what did it matter? She couldn't afford, or even find the time to examine such extras. Life was simple at best. Babies and church—church and babies.

But caring for the children, although tiring, was also enjoyable; and fulfilling. Church work, on the other hand, was hard work. Not to mention living with a man who, at times, seemed to detest her.

The rules of Christian living, published in huge

volumes for referral, were always available as reminders if one strayed from church teachings. Yet that impossibility was laughable as sermons from pulpits across America dictated similar compliance on purity and chaste living—directed mostly at women. The Amen corner often resounded from complacent men who believed wives should remain simple, and unadorned. But did aspiration control undisciplined eyes from lusting after women who were more modern? Well, probably not.

Life was what it was. Overcoming the rules of church leadership and family dictates was always a challenge. But the mistakes others made should never control Hannah's life as they did. Yet it was impossible to change them.

She now realized the man she had married wasn't genuine, God-fearing, or true to his marriage vows. Commitment was a word yet to be defined in his mind. But for her, the bonds of matrimony were to be honored—and celebrated.

But Jeremy's intense hatred continued to slice her heart to bits, denying her one desire for true love and happiness. He now despised his indenture, and became more ingenious, calculating, and destructive as time revealed. His demolition began with personal possessions, and then escalated to body, heart, and soul.

Although fractured early on, Hannah was committed despite numerous red flags indicating her dream marriage had long ago ended. But alienation and manipulation began driving her to re-evaluate her desires, and forcing her into action. It was then she decided to no longer take the abuse. Instead she would seek a way of escape, and flee her abuser permanently—realizing she could never return to a man who enjoyed carving out devastation and ruin in her life.

But her heart had been deceived, and her sanity stripped away. Scars, both physical and emotional, now remained as reminders of past trauma. But once common sense returned, she was thankful that God had not forsaken her. (Deuteronomy 31:6). Belief in Him, and trust in her core values, would see her though.

She wasn't afraid to die. In fact, she no longer feared death as confrontation with that opposition was ongoing. Jeremy's promise to blow her brains out had long before destroyed that fear. In fact, it was implausible at any unexpected moment. However, her concern was for the children. They were worth saving. And, with this in mind, she mentally prepared for what was ahead—her escape to freedom.

A release from her ruined existence would happen. Of this she was certain, or she would die trying. It was simply a matter of time.

Chapter Nine

Baby Times Three

Glancing down, Hannah absentmindedly rubbed her stomach. "I think I might be pregnant," she said, and a hint of a smile formed.

"What?" And instantly Jeremy spun around to face her, fist in hand.

"I said, I think I'm pregnant."

"Get an abortion," he shouted, and his fist pounded the table with unexpected force.

"I can't. It's wrong."

"If you're pregnant I'll tell everyone that baby's not mine."

His words again ripped her heart. But maybe he didn't want his girlfriend to know he was still sleeping with his wife. In her heart Hannah knew he was cheating—long visitations, and late night returns.

"Well, if I am, it was an accident." And she twisted her hands trying to stay calm. "I didn't plan it."

"Get an abortion," he said again, only louder. "I don't want any more kids." Then, with both hands, he clamped the back of his chair. "Two are more than I ever wanted."

"You know I can't get an abortion. It's wrong."

"I don't care. Get one, or get out."

"I haven't even been to the doctor yet," she said, and her lips curved. "I just think I might be."

In the back of her mind she recalled being punched in the stomach when pregnant with Haley, and again with Austin. She would need to be careful. But with a baby on the way, plans to leave the marriage would need to be laid aside. Without a support system in place, or money, any endeavor would be wasted.

And yet, despite the risk, another baby would be exciting. Any diversion in her chaotic life must be a blessing. Perhaps even mend the marriage. Jeremy's infidelity could be forgiven. If only he would be the person he portrayed himself to be—a dedicated minister of the gospel.

The following day Hannah left the doctor's office somewhat elated, but mostly subdued. Could she continue living with an abusive man who didn't want his baby? If only he would change. Her prayer was that things would settle down, and their new addition bring fresh unity to the marriage.

***

Can you help me?" she asked. "Please?"

Jeremy turned, and sauntered across the room. He crossed both arms, then stared down as Hannah cowered on the floor. "What happened to you?"

Still rubbing both ankles, she stared back; and tears began to stream down her cheeks. "I tripped over the threshhold when going outside, and twisted both ankles."

"Well get up," he said. "I'm hungry." He then grabbed a chair, and began tying his shoe laces. "I leave in thirty minutes."

Frightened, she inched over, reached for a chair, and tried to stand. But pulling up was impossible, and she again sank to the floor; writhing in pain. "I can't walk," she said. "I don't even think I can stand."

"Well, that's your problem," he said. But then he rocked forward, causing his chair to lean precariously. "Just because you can't walk doesn't mean you don't take care of things around here."

"Shouldn't I see a doctor?"

"You shouldn't have fallen. Besides, I'm taking the car."

Face now red, he jumped up, and jerked the

refrigerator open. "And since you won't get up," he said, "I'll fix my own sandwich."

The next instant two-year-old Austin tottered through the kitchen, and stopped. "Mama on the floor," he said.

"I know," Hannah said. But her attempt to smile died. "Mama's okay. I just fell, and hurt her legs."

Again she tried to stand, but her ankles were swelling, and screamed resistance. "What about the kids?" she asked.

"You had them. You can take care of them," Jeremy said, a snarl on his face.

She had heard those words before. But why was he so mean hearted?

"I'm out of here," he said, and grabbed his jacket. "Where's my keys?"

"Right there on the table where you left them."

"I don't see them," he barked. "Now get up and help me find them. I'm going to be late."

"I can't walk."

"I need my keys," he said. And his voice rose in decibels with each accelerated word.

Still frightened, Hannah crawled to the table, and fingered the surface. And immediately the clatter of metal against metal jangled in her hand. "Here they are," she said, and lifted them up.

He reached over, grabbed them, and then slammed the door on his way out.

Now seven months pregnant, yet none of Hannah's responsibilities as wife and mother stopped. But no longer did I see herself as marriage partner, but more as caregiver. Jeremy's demeanor had long ago turned sour, making her even more responsible than ever before.

"Austin, honey, go and get your sister," she said. "Tell her I need her." What else could she do? She couldn't walk. But, she could crawl. And, with that in mind, she drew a deep breath, and surrendered to her fate.

"Mama, what happened?" Haley asked, staring down.

"Mama can't walk," Austin said.

At least the babies cared. She wasn't alone after all.

Later, after soaking her ankles, she wrapped them both—all the while praying the pain would ease. Soon she was crawling around on both knees, caring for her babies and the home. Yet her bulging midriff made it difficult to move about. Still she persevered.

"Dear God," she whispered. "Please help the baby not be hurt. I know I fell hard. At least I'm not bleeding."

From sheer determination she learned to manage from her knees—even climbing a tall wooden stool just to reach the stove, and cabinets.

"Dear God, my ankles are throbbing. But, maybe, it's a good thing. Staying on my knees keeps me humble."

"I'm a survivor," she told herself. "If I can work while on my knees, I can do anything."

**

A couple of weeks later, after Hannah was again able to walk, her sisters-in-law stopped by.

"Come on." They were begging. "Go with us."

"I don't want to know."

"We've been talking," Ashley said, and then nudged her sister. "We've heard some things. Something makes us very suspicious—"

"—that Jeremy's fooling around," Emily said, and finished the sentence.

"I don't want to know," Hannah said. "Probably don't need to know either."

"Well, we're still going to find out."

"Okay," Hannah said. "But, don't tell me. I don't want to know."

She didn't have time to learn who Jeremy was having an affair with. She knew she couldn't take care of herself, or the children, without him. She didn't have money of her own, or a job. Besides, she was pregnant. Seven months. What exactly were they thinking?

Days later, as Hannah headed to Ashley's house, nervous reservations again surfaced. "I hope everything goes smooth," she prayed. "And that Ashley's promise not to reveal what she learned about Jeremy be honored."

The children would be staying while Ashley while she visited the gynecologist. At least they were excited.

"We're here," Hannah said, peeking through the screened door. "How's it going?"

"I thought you didn't want to know," Ashley said, and a smile emerged.

"I don't,"

"Okay—then I won't tell you," she said, then held the door open.

"Thanks," Hannah said.

"Hey, kids. Who wants ice cream?" Ashley asked. And instantly they came running; voices babbling and small shoes pounding as they rushed to be first in line.

"Jesse's been excited all morning—since I told him Haley and Austin were coming," Ashley said, after they scampered away.

"They always love playing together," Hannah said, but again shifted in the chair. "I'm glad this family is close, and the kids have each other to play with."

"Me, too," Ashley said.

"Anyway, my doctor's appointment is at three."

"Eight months already, huh?"

"Eight and a half. Seems like forever." And a small sigh erupted. "My stomach's as big as an elephant. I can't even see her feet now."

"I remember when was pregnant," Ashley said, then pulled more popsicles from the freezer. "I'm glad it's you, and not me."

"Three kids are enough," Hannah said, and released a long sigh, "although I would love a dozen."

Ashley laughed again, closed the refrigerator door, and handed Hannah a frozen treat. "You know, when you're pregnant, you can eat as much as you want." And both eyebrows lifted before she licked her own treat.

"Well I guess—if you say so," Hannah said, and then giggled. But minutes later she stood, and reached for her purse. "I need to get on the road. Don't want to be late for the doctor."

"The kids will be fine," Ashley said, as she held the door open. "Trust me. They won't miss you."

"See you later, then."

"Drive careful," Ashley said. "Don't rush, and watch out for traffic."

"Thanks for caring. You're the best," Hannah said, and then waved good-bye.

***

Four weeks later, and shortly after midnight, Matthew presented as an eight pound red-head.

"Hot dog—another boy," Jeremy said before passing out in the hospital hallway.

But again Hannah was content. Mothering came natural for her. A baby at her breast and two tagalongs were the happiest days of her life.

Chapter Ten

Just Fix It

"Everything's your fault," Jeremy said, staring at Hannah. More spiteful words, spoken in anger, then rolled from his lips. Yet how many times had she been blamed for what was not her fault? She turned away, and rolled her eyes in disgust. What had she done now?

"What's this?" he asked, and threw a newly ripped envelope at her.

She caught the paper, and quickly scanned the contents. "Your decreased house payment hasn't been approved for the current year," she said, reading the letter. Then she drew a sharp breath. *This revelation could be costly, and we can't afford a higher payment.*

Jeremy plopped down on a nearby chair, and stared at her—eyes flashing. Then he raised his eyebrows. "Exactly what does that mean?" he asked.

The words were repeated, but more slowly.

"What?" And he bolted upright.

"Read the letter," she said, pointing to the paper in her hand.

"You're supposed to keep up with this stuff."

"I don't know what it means," she said. Then realizing his rage was rising, she again responded; this time in softer tones. "I'll call them and see what I can do."

"You'd better take care of this quick," he said, eyes again flashing. "And, I mean today." Still angry, he jerked his jacket off the back of his chair, and stomped outside.

But as soon as the door slammed, Haley and Austin

came running. At least, for now, they were too young to understand their dad's temperament. However, by the time Jeremy was again home, Hannah's stomach was tied in knots. Although she dreaded relating the news, truth is truth.   "Our house payment is going to double," she said.

"Why?"

"Because we didn't file the proper paperwork this year."

"Why didn't you take care of this before it happened?" he asked, and then swatted at her.

"I—I didn't know," she said, then quickly placed the baby in his high chair for safe keeping; all the while breathing a quick prayer for protection.

"You're supposed to know," he said, and his face blazed. "I don't have time for this."

"No paperwork came in the mail."

"You're supposed to take care of things like this."

"I didn't know anything about it."

"Then get a job," he said, and a scowl replaced his frown. "We need more money."

"I can't get a job. We have three little kids."

"That's your problem, not mine," he said.

The next instant he was pacing the floor, and his anger seemed to increase with each stomp of the foot.

Still frightened, Hannah tried to redirect his rage, fearing yet another beating. "You promised I could stay home and take care of the kids," she said, cowering.

"I've changed my mind," he said, and his face again reddened.

"If I get a job, the cost of daycare will take everything I make."

"I don't care," he said, and stomped even harder to emphasis his words. "I said, get a job. I can't keep supporting you, and the kids, on church salary and my other job."

"That makes no sense," she said, then grabbed a piece of scrap paper to write on. "Look at the numbers. There's no way working a job right now will help anything. We have three pre-school age kids. Daycare would eat up my paycheck. Besides, we wanted the children to learn principals from us, and not a babysitter." Still frightened, she took a deep breath, and waited.

"Well, we have to do something," he said, "or we'll lose the house."

"I'll—I'll talk to the bank again," was all she could say.

But the answer was the same. They would be selling their home, and moving to a less expensive house. Jeremy's salary wasn't enough to keep their heads above water.

***

Moving day was hectic as Hannah skirted about, trying to keep peace between three rambunctious children and a super-sensitive husband. Matthew, now an active toddler, meandered among assorted items in his room ready for boxing up. Haley, toys piled in colorful heaps, sorted through various dolls and accessories for transporting to their new home. Jeremy, on the other hand, dragged two large suitcases into the living room, and sat them on end in the middle of the floor. He then left the room.

Minutes later Austin darted through a wide opening between kitchen and living room in an attempt to leap over the cases. His terrifying screams instantly brought Hannah on a run. A sharp piece of glass from the now broken storm door had embedded above one of his knees. Blood squirted from the wound, and his leg was covered in streams of sticky red.

"Call 911," she yelled; then grabbed Austin, ran to the kitchen, and snatched up the phone. But Jeremy was nowhere to be found.

Phone in hand, she punched in 911. "Come quick," she said. "My three-year-old has a piece of glass in his leg, and blood is squirting everywhere.

Shortly after the call a rescue team arrived amid sirens and clanging bells. The glass shards were then removed, and a compress applied. "He needs to go to the emergency room and get stitched up," one of rescuers said, patting Austin on the head. "We don't stitch wounds. We only stop the bleeding."

"I can't thank you enough," Hannah said, but her heart continued to pound.

Seconds later Jeremy sauntered in the room. "Why are they here?" he asked, and pointed outside.

"You know those suitcases you left in the middle of the floor?"

"Yes?"

"Austin knocked them over, fell through the storm door, and it shattered." Her hands, now wet with sweat, were rubbed together. "We need to take him to the hospital for stitches. He had glass in his leg. He's bleeding."

"You should've been watching him."

"Why did you leave those suitcases in the middle of the floor?"

"Shut up. Just shut up," he said, and his fist clinched. But his words seemed to mock and criticize at the same time.

"Can you drive us to the hospital?"

"I'm not going anywhere," he said. "I'm busy packing. We're moving, remember?"

"Can you watch Haley and Matthew?"

"No. Take them with you."

Hannah knew better than to argue.

"Come on, kids," she said. "Let's take your brother to the emergency room for stitches."

Chapter Eleven

Sandbox Debacle

Now settled from their recent move, Hannah could only pray Jeremy's stress level would drop, and things at home be more relaxed. Losing the house, and living in another, was a small price to pay if their marriage improved.

But things only grew worse, and she soon felt the pressure of more volatile responses. Jeremy's appetite to climb an advanced ladder in the church conference arena, and make a bigger name for himself, only enhanced his aggravated status. Now more callas than before, his behavior escalated to new levels of rage; but always at another's expense.

***

In a rare moment of time Jeremy decided to watch the children while at play. But a loud cry from the sandbox brought new panic to Hannah's heart, and she raced to the porch. However, when she tried to brush past, he reached his arm out, and stopped her.

"I'll go," he said. He turned, sauntered to the sandbox, and lifted Matthew from the sand. He then returned to the porch. Meanwhile Haley and Austin, oblivious to the baby's cries, continued to play nearby.

"His diaper's wet, and he's rubbing his eyes," Jeremy said.

"I'll take him," Hannah said. But as she reached out, memories of past roughness surfaced in her mind.

"No, I can handle it," he said; then sat down, still holding Matthew, who continued to cry.

"Shut up—shut up," he said in response; then forced the baby down on the cement porch, where more squalls erupted.

"Please, let me take him," Hannah said, heart in throat.

"I said I'd handle it," Jeremy said, then swatted at the sand in the baby's eyes. But Matthew only wailed louder.

"Get me a wet washcloth," Jeremy said.

"That will only make it worse."

"I said, get me a wet rag."

The tone in his voice was strong, emphasizing his demand, and she was instantly terrified. Still feeling defenseless, she returned with the cloth. But her heart quaked with dread.

Now unable to watch, she turned away; knowing one doesn't apply anything wet to dry sand without expecting a disaster. And instantly Matthew's screams ripped her heart to shreds.

"I told you," she said. "Anything wet only makes it worse." Then she stepped back, but remained cautious; dreading the worst.

"Shut up, you ugly bitch," Jeremy said; then grabbed Matthew, turned him over, and spanked him with hands of steel.

"Please God—please help Matthew."

Again, in blind faith, she reached for the baby. But in an unexpected move, Jeremy stood, and shoved him into her arms.

"Here," he said. "You take him." Then, with a scowl on his face, he turned on his heel, and headed to the car. "I'm leaving now," he growled. "I don't like stupid kids." The door then slammed, tires squealed, and he was gone.

Immediately Hannah ran inside for a dry cloth.

Minutes later, and now dry from top to bottom, Matthew's cries smoldered to sniffles. Hannah, more than grateful things had turned out okay, again thanked God for wisdom on removing wet sand from a child's eyes.

Chapter Twelve

Merciless Driver

"Get in. We're late."

Jeremy's undisciplined bark was enough to send Hannah into a tailspin. It was her responsibility, however, to help the children into their car seats before climbing into hers. Still she huddled into herself—just in case. But after they were secured, all but one leg remained when a gust of wind blew past, the door vibrated, and the car squealed from the curb.

"You're making me late," Jeremy said after the door swung shut with Hannah barely inside. "And couldn't you find anything better to wear than that?" he asked, pointing at her dress. "You look like an old hag."

"It's the best I have," she said, still winded. Then trying to hide her embarrassment, she smoothed the top of her outdated dress while recalling his recently purchased suit and tie.

"Well, wear something better next time," he said. "You make me look bad." And he jerked the steering wheel to emphasize his words. "Better yet, do something with that ugly hair."

Fire instantly blazed across her face. *I'm doing the best I can. You're the only one who gets new things in this family.*

Meanwhile he accelerated his way through town, and she grabbed the arm rest for support. Still frenzied, he raced through two red lights before the road widened into the main drag. His rage was now out of control.

Then, as the car began its incline, she methodically analyzed the sharp curves ahead. Every bump and pothole seemed to accentuate the narrowness of the road as they rushed headlong up the mountain. Loud profanity and vulgar insinuations flowed from his lips as easily as did his sermons. But why couldn't others see him as she did?

The next instant he turned the car toward a ravine, all the while sneering and cursing. "We'll never make it by seven," he said. But his words, spit through pursed lips, destroyed all confidence as the unsteady car slid away from the edge of a precipice; and just in the nick of time.

"Please, please be careful," Hannah said, still shaking. Could he get any angrier? Dread in the form of a knot was creeping up her throat. Meanwhile, the kids randomly cried out in fear and pain as they methodically slammed into each other.

Again shifting in the seat, she positioned for another hard slam against the door. Bruises forming beneath her skin now throbbed from a crushing jolt just seconds before. The car then blazed through a wide curve, and slid toward the edge of a deep gorge. *Please help us, Lord.*

Her heart again raced as Jeremy jerked the car back. Yet it continued to swerve, weaving and swaying back and forth under the duress of speed. She prayed we would make it to church.

Tires screeched a reminder of unknown horrors as they whiplashed back and forth in the veering car. Spiteful out-of-control maneuvers and vicious language rattled her brain. She cringed at his innuendos.

Still frightened, she reached behind the seat and steadied the baby's lopsided car seat. What else could she do? She feared for all of them.

But as the crazed auto swiped past a border of prickly brambles close to the gorge, she grabbed her throat. "Please slow down. Please,"

"Shut up, you mother-fucking bitch." His words were cold. And still the car raced upward. But when they reached the pinnacle, huge boulders and massive crevice rose up from below—as if to defy them.

Jeremy's out-of-control rage then spurred them downward—the car weaving and swaying relentlessly on a dangerous trek toward church. Hateful, menacing words again shred her heart, as his actions held them captive. But as if divinely orchestrated, the brakes slammed, and they had arrived.

With a shove of the hand, he yanked the shaft into park, jerked the door open, and stepped outside. "Good to see you this evening, Brother Ralph," he said, extending his hand to a seasoned church member.

For Hannah—well she was more than happy to place shaky feet on solid ground again; even more thankful Jeremy's haste and recklessness hadn't landed them all at the bottom of a ravine.

***

The following week seemed to fly by, and it was again Sunday. But after church that same morning Jeremy insisted they accept a church member's invitation, and spend the day with them. Although Hannah dreaded caring for small children away from home, it was easier to comply than to argue.

But at long last, the day ended; and she could again breathe easier. Parental responsibility had all been hers, and she was exhausted.

"God is our refuge and strength, a very present help in trouble." Powerful words repeated again and again helped to calm her spirit, and refresh her mind.

Again home, she plopped into bed, and pulled the blankets over her worn out body. Just the thought of sleeping children eased her mind, and she released a long sigh of relief. It was time for some much needed rest. Then, as she sank deep into the comforter, she resigned to the solace of fatigue. Could she do another thing? Well, probably not.

The next instant a door slammed, and heavy footsteps roused her. Jeremy was in the room.

He tossed his shirt and jacket on the foot of the bed, and then cleared his throat. "Why don't you get up and make me something to eat?" he asked.

"I'm really tired," she said, and her eyelids drooped after a fleeting glance through slanted lids. "We've been gone all day."

"Well, I'm hungry," he said, yet continued standing in the doorway, hands on hips.

"Can't you make your own sandwich this time?"

"You know I don't know where anything is. Besides, I'm tired too, you damn bitch. I preached twice today, remember?"

"Can I skip it this time?" she asked. And her lids again sagged. "I watched the kids all day by myself."

"Wasn't my fault."

Heavy footsteps then tromped to the door, a switch clicked, and the room illuminated. The next instant she squeezed her eyes tight, and tried to block the light as unexpected brightness often gave her migraines. But an aura of fog surrounded her, and that ever-gnawing ache of head pain began to slowly settle in.

Jeremy's voice now echoed from down the hallway; and she struggled to sit up.

"Wake up, kids," he said. "Time to get up, and play with your toys."

The haze around Hannah swirled and mocked as she crawled from bed, and stumbled down the hallway; still rubbing her head. "What are you doing?" she asked.

"Time to get up," Jeremy said, shaking Austin by the shoulder. "Wake up, little buddy. Get up and play."

"Please don't," she said, still blinking, as Jeremy lifted a toy truck and waved it in the air.

"Look Matthew. See what Daddy's got? Don't you want to play?"

Matthew stretched, and then opened eyes.

"Hey, Mama wants to play with you," Jeremy said.

Reaching out, Hannah grabbed Jeremy's arm. "Please stop," she said. "They need their sleep."

But he flung her hand away. "Get up," he said, again shaking Austin's shoulder. "Don't you want to play? It's time to play."

"Please don't wake them. Please." Still her head continued to spin, so she closed her eyes; only to open them again when Jeremy's laughter resounded from Haley's room. "Wake up, Haley," he said. "It's time to play."

"Please stop," Hannah said, after stepping through her door. She reached out, and then grabbed his arm; but quickly dropped it when she was pinched.

"Look Haley," Jeremy said. "Mama wants to play with you."

Still rubbing her eyes, Haley sat up in bed, and yawned.

"Get up, Haley—time to play. Don't you want to play?" Jeremy's tainted words, unrelenting and sharp, echoed through the house. But his look was taunting, and Hannah winced at his demeanor.

But the boy's cries again caught her attention, and she turned away. Jeremy, not to be outdone, grabbed her by the hair; and she stopped dead in her tracks.

"Where do you think you're going?" he asked.

"The boys are crying."

"So what?"

"I don't like them crying."

"Do they need their mommy?" he asked in a tone that both mocked and heckled.

The next instant she jerked free of his grasp and hobbled away. Still the snickering continued.

But once in the boy's room she lifted Matthew from the crib; then rushed to Austin's bed. "It's okay," she said in a soothing tone. "Shhh."

Still trying to calm them, she patted Austin on the head. "Lay back down," she said. And again she whispered. "It's alright. Go back to sleep."

Austin stared up from the pillow, eyes brimming. And

then her own eyes filled. *Oh, God. Please help me. My head is pounding, and I can't see through this migraine. What am I going to do? Oh, God, please help me know what to do.*

In the background Jeremy's car keys jangled against each other. The next instant the outside door slammed, and Hannah breathed a deep sigh of relief.

Thank God he's gone. But here I am again, calming everyone down. Will it always be this way?

Hannah needed help—but where could she find it? Jeremy's family would never accept the fact that he was mean to his family. And neither would hers. And, heaven forbid, she tell anyone at church. Besides, they wouldn't believe her. Jeremy was too charismatic to discredit.

She closed her eyes, and squeezed back her swollen tears. *Where does he go anyway when he leaves the house? And do I really care?*

Then, as she held her bursting head, she allowed the tears to flow at will.

Chapter Thirteen

Life on the Edge

Jeremy's car sputtered and stopped; and then the car door slammed. Half afraid, and somewhat panicked, Hannah scurried to the living room, and prepared to greet him. "You're home early," she said as he came through the door.

But without one word in response, he flung his jacket at the sofa, turned, and glared at her.

"Dinner's ready if you're hungry," she said, backing away.

He grimaced, reached back, and slammed the door shut. "What is it?" he grumbled before throwing his car keys on a table near the door. He then kicked the cat to the wall, and sauntered toward the kitchen.

Abrasive grinding advised he was scraping his chair across the tiles toward the table. A silent prayer was again lifted as she hung his jacket on a hook, took a gulp of air, and hurried to the kitchen.

"Today I made spaghetti," she said, but her gut was choking on fear. Then, after a quick glance at the floor, she heaped a large spoonful of noodles and sweet-smelling sauce onto a clean plate.

The earsplitting sound of metal scraping wood immediately sent shivers up and down her spine. The next instant he bolted from the table, grabbed his plate and, in one quick jerk, hurled the contents to the ceiling.

Out of instinct she recoiled as meat and noodles crashed to the floor in a tangled heap. Her well-planned meal was now peeling off the splattered ceiling—leaving a sticky trail on its way down to the floor.

"Clean it up," he said, teeth gritted and fist clinched. "Clean it up now." Then he shook his fist, and more words erupted—all laced with profanity.

Frightened, she grabbed a soft cloth, stooped down, and began to wipe the oozing mess off the now greasy floor. In the background his eerie laughter kept her on edge.

The next instant a chair scraped the floor, and he began to pace the small kitchen, corner to corner. An avalanche of insults and profanity rolled from his lips nonstop as he mythically beat his fists together.

"You'd better get this mess cleaned up before I get back," he said. His words, raw and course, struck a new cord of terror in Hannah's heart; and demanded instant obedience.

Again looking up, she noted a triumphant smirk on his face. But when he caught her eye, his flashed. "I'm going to Hardee's and get some real food," he said. He turned on his heel, and then tramped to the next room.

"Where's my keys?" he asked. But his words, spoken through gritted teeth, were explosive.

Still terrorized, Hannah stood from her crouched position on the floor. "Right there on the table where you left them," she said. Yet her words were weak, as the disaster around her was more than unsettling. Heavy footsteps and the rattle of metal jarred her thoughts. A loud crash followed.

"Keep this stuff out of her way," he said. His words were spat, yet seemed to reverberate through the house.

Her flight to the next room was swift.

Seventeen-month-old Matthew was huddled near his new wheelie. The handlebar was bent, and the wheels dislocated. A gust of air blew past when a tightened fist swatted her face. "You'd better not buy him another one," Jeremy said, hands clinched.

Another prayer was lifted after he stomped to the door. The next instant he jerked it open, still uttering vulgarity, and stepped outside.

Matthew's lips puckered as Hannah lifted him in her arms. Then, with a gentle hand, she rubbed his head followed by a kiss. Still holding him close, she carried him to the bedroom. "Where are my other two?" she asked, searching with her eyes.

"This is becoming more and more frequent," she whispered under her breath. But as if she already knew, she reached behind the bed for Austin. "You can come out now," she said. "Everything's going to be all right. I promise."

The sound of running feet then caught her attention, and she turned as Haley sprinted into the room; a questioning look on her face.

"Don't worry, Haley. Daddy's gone for now," Hannah said, and wrapped her arms around her daughter. "Always remember. God will take care of us."

Words recently read in the Bible then popped into her mind. "The righteous cry out, and the LORD hears them; He delivers them from all their troubles" (Psalms 34:17) and "...be strong in the LORD and in his mighty power" (Ephesians 6:10). After that she was comforted.

***

The following afternoon Jeremy's car rolled to the curb in front of the house, and stopped. A huge lump then formed in Hannah's throat, and she took a staggered breath. "Please God," she whispered. "Help him be in a good mood. This love-hate scenario is getting harder and harder to understand."

Still she knew better than to ask where he had been all night. Deep breaths kept her calm as she recalled the difficulties of scrubbing spattered spaghetti from furniture, cabinets, and tiny crevices in the kitchen. *He may still be mad. I don't know—*

Loud, thumping footsteps outside the kitchen door accelerated her need to seek cover. The next instant she slipped between the door and refrigerator, her place of refuge when Jeremy came home in a foul mood; which was more and more frequent as time revealed.

It seemed the children also reserved a place to hide. Austin would scoot behind his bed, and Haley would slip to her room, close the door, and play in silence. The baby just toddled around, often in harm's way. But, that's just the way it was.

The next instant the door flung open, and a burst of hot air gushed inside. Jeremy then reached for Hannah, and pulled her out. "What are you doing in that corner?" he asked.

"Looking out the window, I guess," she said. But the corner of her shirt dangled after it dropped—twisted out of shape by nervous fingers as his mood was analyzed.

"Let's go downtown and get some ice cream," he said. He then grabbed Haley; and swung her around. "What do you guys think?"

"Swing me too, Daddy. Swing me." And the younger ones lifted their arms, for once unafraid.

All Hannah could do was to swallow her pride, and brush her worries aside. "I guess we could," flowed from her lips as she pulled her skirt straight, and pressed the wrinkles flat with her hands.

"Well, come on," he said. "Let's go." He hoisted Haley to his shoulders, and then headed to the car. Austin followed close behind.

A silent prayer was again lifted as Hannah shifted Matthew to her hip, and locked the door. "Please God. Please help Jeremy not get mad at me, or the kids," she prayed. "And please, please keep us safe."

"I guess I'll put on her happy face," she whispered in Matthew's tiny ear. "Who knows? Maybe things will get better after all."

Chapter Fourteen

Syrup of Ipecac

After slipping a thick coat on, Hannah stood in the doorway and waited for Jeremy to glance her way; realizing his attention span was as limited as his ability to respond.

"Can you watch the kids about fifteen minutes?" she asked.

"Noooo—don't throw the ball," he said, snapping his fingers as if to hurry the football players on the television screen. His muscles then flexed in agitated response.

"Please. I'll be quick. It's too cold to take them out for milk and bread."

"What?" Again he glanced up, but quickly refocused on the action at hand.

"I need to run to the store. I'll only be gone a few minutes. It's too cold to take the kids out in the snow."

"Okay, okay."

"They're playing in the bedroom," she said, all the while watching for a facial response. There was none. "Are you listening?"

"Huh? Yeah."

"Are you sure? I'll take them with me if you don't want to watch them."

"Go on. They'll be fine."

"I'll hurry," she said. Then, in a flash, she ran to the car and sped to the store. Working fast, she grabbed the needed items, and accelerated back home. But when she opened the kitchen door, her heart leaped to her throat. Both boys were squatted on the floor. But Austin had a look of guilt on his face. Matthew, beside him, was holding an empty bottle of children's vitamins in his hand; and eating one.   Terrified, Hannah dropped the grocery bag on the counter, and grabbed the bottle. "What are you eating?" she asked, again staring at a dark purple residue swathing the slobbery mouths of both boys. Then she grabbed the bottle, and read a black label glued to the bottom of the container. The warning cautioned consumers of iron poisoning if more than one vitamin was ingested each day.

"Quick. Call Poison Control."

"I'm glad you're back," Jeremy said, meandering to the kitchen.

"You don't know?" she asked, hands on hips. "You didn't watch them, did you?"

"You were gone too long."

"I wasn't gone long at all," she said; then dropped her coat on a chair, turned, and grabbed the phone. "I can't believe you let them eat vitamins. Why didn't you give them a cookie, or something?"

"Why didn't you take them with you?"

"You promised to watch them."

"You had them. They're your problem, not mine," he said. And, with a look of arrogance, turned, and left the room. But, seconds later, he returned with his coat.

"I just called Poison Control," she said, in measured tone. "They told me to give them both Syrup of Ipecac, and make them throw up." Again her voice trembled. "I hope it's not too late."

"What do you mean?"

"This syrup is for people who swallow poisons, and need to throw them up."

Jeremy pulled his coat on, turned, and swung the kitchen door open. "Well, I'm not helping with that," he said. Cold air swept past as the door slammed shut.

Why won't he ever help me? And why is it always just me? But, she didn't have time to worry.

What can I do? What can I do?

Panicked, she ran to the bathroom and jerked the

medicine cabinet open. Inside was a recently purchased bottle of Syrup of Ipecac. "Thank God," she whispered. *But how can I do this by myself?*

"I'll call Jeremy's sister," she said out loud. "Maybe she'll come over and help me."

Minutes later the bathroom sported a stained array of cotton towels covered in sticky fragments of purple residue. Exhausted, but triumphant, Emily and Hannah plopped down on separate kitchen chairs as two messy boys, shirts more stained than before, gobbled down bowls of cold cereal with their sister.

"At least they're okay," Hannah said, at last relieved.

"I'm just glad I was home, and could help," Emily said. She then stood, and straightened the top button on her coat. "Are you leaving?"

"I need to run," Emily said. "It's getting late."

"Thanks for helping," Hannah said, and a smile broke through. "Jeremy didn't want to."

"Well, it's over now," Emily said, "and everything is back to normal."

"Yes, I guess it is."

Then, in quick exchange, Hannah slid her chair back, and stepped to the door—arms extended. "Thanks, again, Sissy," she said, and gave her a quick hug. "I knew I could count on you. You're the best."

Chapter Fifteen

Skating to Disaster

Haley and Austin had been invited for an evening at the local skating rink. In fact, all the youth from church were going. Everyone able to don a pair of skates and tackle the challenges of wheel balancing had been invited. Designated for local churches, this event had been meticulously planned. Christian music would highlight the evening for skaters doing their rounds on the floor. And, at Haley's insistence, Hannah also donned a pair of skates; ready to test her endurance with the other skaters.

Austin, somewhat hesitant, edged out on the floor. Haley, more exuberant than he, rolled ahead with the older kids. Matthew, too young to skate, was spending time with Mrs. Allen, whom he called Grams.

But for Hannah, trying to stay balanced was a disaster in the making after the floor filled with skaters. When she ventured out on the floor, a caravan rushed past at break-neck speed. A strong arm then struck her from behind, and she was instantly facing the floor. Her attempt to look steady on wheels had failed.

Splintering throbs from elbow to hand then exploded through her left limb. Yet leaving the floor was impossible as untold agony was sending her adrift with each beat of the heart.

Yet the torture only increased, and she found herself slipping in and out of consciousness. Oblivious to those around her, she was dragged from the floor. But as cold air from the outside drifted inside through a crack in the door, her body began to shake uncontrollably.

"I'm going to faint," she whispered. "Somebody please help. I'm going to faint."

"You need to go to the hospital," a voice said. "I think your arm is broken."

Realizing it was Ashley, Hannah opened her eyes. "What about the kids?" she asked. But her words were muffled, and distant.

"We'll take them to the hospital with us," Ashley said.

Then, as Hannah watched through blurry eyes, Ashley grabbed several coats from a nearby chair and tossed them at a small group huddled near the door. After that her eyes refused to focus, and she drifted in and out of consciousness.

Minutes later Ashley grabbed her by the arm, helped her to stand, and then pushed her to the car. Still holding Ashley's arm, she staggered through the hospital entrance; still overcome with pain. The children followed close behind.

***

"Your left wrist is broken, and your elbow is fractured," the doctor said after pointing to X-rays pictured on the screen. But Hannah barely heard his words as darkness folded in around her.

Doctor and nurse, working together, then pulled the bone sitting atop her hand back down into the wrist fragment, allowing the ridges of both arm and hand to meet. *Lamaze—Lamaze breaths. Oh God, it hurts.*

"I'll seal the cast on your arm and elbow," the doctor said, when Hannah again opened her eyes.

Still confused, she stared back.

"You'll need to wear this cast at least six weeks," he said.

Six weeks? How could she possibly live in a cast for six weeks?

"How do you feel?"

"Much better after you put my arm back together," she said.

"Well, that's good," he said, a smile of sympathy on his face. "Take some aspirin for the pain, and I'll see you again in two weeks."

A long sigh escaped. But, somehow, she would manage. Everyone depended on her

But once home she staggered through the door and flopped down on a sofa. Then she looked at Jeremy, who only grunted in response to her appearance. "I broke her arm tonight," she said, and new tears formed.

He glanced up, but then his eyes returned to the television screen. "Well, you shouldn't have gone skating," he said. His voice lacked emotion.

"But, it was church night, and the kids wanted to go. Besides, I didn't know I'd break her arm."

"Well, you're on your own," he said. He then stood, face immobile, as Haley and Austin rushed through the door.

"Mama broke her arm," Haley said, gasping for air as she pealed her coat off and threw it on the sofa.

"Pick it up and go to bed," Jeremy said. But the sternness in his voice, and the look on his face, instantly sent both children packing to the back of the house.

"Where's the baby?"

Ashley's keeping him tonight," Hannah said. "She'll bring him by in the morning."

"So, what happened?"

"I was knocked down at the skating rink. But when I fell, I broke my wrist, and fractured my elbow."

"Well, too bad for you," he said; and his head moved back and forth in a mocking way.

"It hurts," she said, still holding the cast close. "The doctor told me to take aspirin for the pain. But, I don't think it helps much."

"Well, get them yourself," he said.

Still, his lack of emotion was hurtful, and she desired more concern. Yet she wasn't surprised at his disdain, although she dreaded the struggle as it was obvious he truly didn't care. His next words jerked her back to reality.

"As for the kids—you had them," he said, and lunged at her. "You can take care of them."

The next instant he and his keys were out the door. The engine roared, and he was gone—at least for a time.

"Thank God he's gone," she said under her breath as she stumbled to the kitchen; still gripping the cast.

"Hey, kids—anybody hungry?" she asked. And immediately they ran to the kitchen, bumping into each other on the way. Austin, with a nervous eye, glanced around the room. "Where's Daddy?" he asked.

"Gone somewhere," Hannah said, trying to smile. But it was impossible. The pain was just too great. Yet, responsibility was important, so she pressed onward. "How about a quick snack before bedtime?"

Again struggling for strength and composure, Hannah ripped open a new bag of loaf bread with her free hand. And, with that same hand, she slapped peanut butter and jelly on one slice, and placed the other on top.

"I'm sorry it's so sloppy," she said, then handed half to each child after it was haphazardly sliced. "I'll read one short story each, and then its bedtime, for real."

Could she survive the pain? Six weeks was a very long time.

Again her body sagged as elbow and wrist continued to throb. But having only one hand to work with was an indication of what was ahead.

***

It was impossible to lay flat. Hannah's arm and wrist throbbed incessantly—the pain so severe the doctor's suggestion of sleeping in an upright position now sounded realistic.

She glanced around the room, and her eyes landed on Jeremy's recliner. It looked inviting enough. Besides, he wouldn't care if she slept in his bed, or not.

But with only one functioning hand, everything would be a challenge. Cast or no cast, life would continue—with or without assistance. Taking care of the kids would be a real test. Jeremy wouldn't help. His family couldn't. It would also be the same with church members. Again it was just Hannah—stuck between a rock and a hard place.

And, as expected, Jeremy didn't bat an eye at her struggles, or her pain. He didn't flinch even once at her hardship. His rhetorical laughter often resounded to the rooftops at her disposition. However, his disdain for her temporary disability was noted, and tucked away for future reference.

***

When she stepped outside the doctor's office following a six-week check-up, Hannah allowed the tears to flow once more. She would be wearing the cast at least two more weeks. Her wrist wasn't healing fast enough to please him.

But two weeks later, he was all smiles.

"I didn't want to tell you eight weeks ago," he said, "but I was afraid your wrist wouldn't heal properly." Again he smiled. "But, it did. You're one lucky lady."

Chapter Sixteen

A Real Princess

Jeremy's actions again brought Hannah on a run—this time to the back porch. "What are you doing?" she asked. But her words were more of a gasp. In his hand was a pistol.

"I don't want that dog anymore," he said. "Now get out of my way." Then, with face set, he turned, shoved her toward the wall, and strode outside.

Princess, a beautiful blue-eyed Husky, began to wag her tail as he walked toward her. But the attached chain was tangled so she remained in her place; still wagging her tail.

The dog, a gift to Jeremy from Rick, Emily's husband, only added to Hannah's workload. Still, the children gave her as much love and attention as possible. But, a dog in chains was one thing. Killing her was another.

"Please don't kill her," she said, catching up; and then moving closer. Still concerned, she reached out, and gingerly touched his shoulder. "Princess didn't do anything wrong. She's a good dog."

"I said I don't want that dog anymore," he said, and his teeth gritted. He grunted, aimed the pistol, and a shot rang out. And instantly the dog let out a yelp.

Hannah's heart was now in her throat. How could he do such a thing?

"Please, stop," she said, and squeezed her eyes tight; trying to stop the flow of tears. "Please don't shoot again— please."

Sweat moistened her upper lip as the dog whimpered, and pulled against the chains. She still feared for the dog's life.

"Please stop—don't kill her," Hannah begged. "Please."

"Get out of my way," Jeremy said, and his eyes blazed. "Just get out of my way."

"Princess can be fixed," Hannah whispered. "I know she can. I'll take her to a vet. He'll remove the bullet. She'll be okay."

But when another shot rang out, the dog again thrashed about, yelping in pain. Blood gushed from her shattered thigh, and then drizzled to the ground; and Hannah's heart again ripped into shreds. Yet before she could move, another bullet whirred past. This time it splintered a dogwood tree. "Please stop," she said.

Now weak, she leaned up against the porch rail, still pleading. But the sound of death again whirled past, and a third bullet hit Princess square in the jaw.

"I'm out of bullets," Jeremy said, a cruel smirk on his face. He turned, shot Hannah a look of disdain, and then hurried inside.

Still following close behind, Hannah continued to beg for the dog's life. "What about Princess?" she asked. "She needs a doctor." She needed to stay calm—for the dog.

"I'm not doing anything for that dog," he said, and his lip curled. "I'll call Rick. He can finish her off."

Tears continued to cascade down Hannah's cheeks, and she leaned against the wall for support. "Please."

"Don't do anything for that dog," he said, and his tone demanded obedience. "I mean it. Leave her alone."

"What about the kids?"

"Don't tell the kids."

***

Later that same evening, after everyone was in bed, Hannah's eyes refused to close. Princess, outside the bedroom window, whimpered and cried out through the night; and her heart was broken for her. Jeremy's actions had been cruel, and Hannah struggled with the consequences.

What can I do without him turning on me? If I take Princess to the vet, I'll get in trouble. But if I do nothing, she'll die. What if he turns the gun on me?

The next day Rick dragged the dog to his truck, and drove away. But as the truck rambled past, Hannah's heart again broke in two. At least Princess would soon be out of her misery.

Words from the Bible then filtered through her head.

"A righteous man cares for the needs of his animal, but the kindest acts of the wicked are cruel" (Proverbs 12:10)

But at that moment, Hannah didn't yet know those canine eyes of blue would haunt her for years to come.

***

"I'm putting the big television on the boy's bureau," Jeremy said several days later, and then continued his stride down the hallway. In his arms was the oversized set.

"At least he's in a good mood for a change," Hannah whispered, then followed close behind. But once in the room she glanced up at the tall furniture, and gasped. "Don't you think this bureau is too high? The boys might pull it over when reaching up."

"Well, that's where it's going," Jeremy said, and then lifted the set to the top before scooting it to the middle of the furniture. "I'm only doing this once. It'd better stay put."

"I still think it's too tall for that television set."

"Don't worry about it."

Minutes later a deafening crash echoed from down the hallway. Hannah, heart in throat, dropped the laundry basket, and raced back to the bedroom. She mentally prepared for the worst.

But once in the room she found Matthew crawling out from beneath the bureau. A large gash on his forehead gushed blood, and he was crying incessantly. Austin, mouth gaping wide, was standing to the side. The set itself lay in two pieces on the floor, tubes exposed, and the face cracked in several places. Assorted piles of clothing from lopsided, half-opened drawers haphazardly spilled to the floor in colorful piles of cotton.

Panicked, she grabbed a tee from an open drawer, and quickly dabbed the cut on Matthew's head. "Jeremy. Where are you?" she asked, her voice rising. "Come here. Quick." *What is taking him so long?*

Haley, now in the room, was crying as Jeremy strolled in. "Well, now they won't have a TV anymore, will they?" he asked. But his words, accusatory and cold, were unfeeling.

Although frightened, Hannah ignored his comment, and pressed on. "I think Matthew needs stitches," she said.

"You shouldn't have left them alone," Jeremy said, a sneer on his face. He turned, still angry, and kicked the broken set a couple of times before stomping from the room.

"We need to take Matthew to the emergency room," Hannah yelled.

No answer.

"Aren't you going to help?"

"You take care of it," he yelled back. The door then slammed, the car revved, and he was gone.

Matthew continued to whimper as the cloth on his wound turned crimson red. Again Hannah re-wrapped the cut, and then lifted him in her arms.

"Austin. Hurry up and get in the car. Haley, grab my purse, and hold the door open. I need to take your brother to the hospital."

"What happened to the love Jeremy and I once embraced?" she whispered. "Unforgettable moments while contemplating new rendezvous together? Lips pursed, and ready to kiss at all times? Faithful and unified while serving God—anticipating lives together with nothing but love to steer us forward. Where did it all go? Exactly when did it end?"

Overcome with emotion, Hannah dropped her head, and cried bitter tears.

Chapter Seventeen

Obsessed

"Come in here," Jeremy said; voice tense—words demanding.

Dreading what was ahead, Hannah cautiously entered the living room. "I don't think this is going to be a good thing," she whispered.

He glanced up, and then motioned her over. "I rented a movie for tonight," he said.

"What movie?" she asked, and then looked down. The letters XXX leaped out from the cover of a black and white case, now opened and positioned on the table. "Is this a porno movie?"

"Sit down," he said. "You need to watch it with me."

"I don't want to watch it," she said, and took two steps back. "I don't think you should either."

"I'm watching it, and so are you."

"No, I'm not."

"I said you are. Now get over here."

"I don't want to watch," she said, and again edged toward the hallway.

"This will make their marriage better," he said. But then his eyes glazed, and she noted a wine cooler in his hand.

He never drinks this stuff. What is he doing?

"What if the kids wake up?" she asked; then glanced back down the hall while her brain scrambled for more excuses.

"They won't." "I really don't want to watch that movie. I'm tired," she said, and tried to cover a yawn; but it went unnoticed. At this point, all Hannah could do was pray he would leave her alone.

"Sit down," he said. But his words, raw and bold, demanded compliance. He then waved a pre-made fist in the air.

"Please. I don't like stuff like this."

"I said get over here," he said. "Now."

There wasn't any way around his demand. He meant business. Then, as fear enveloped her heart, she stepped to the sofa, and gingerly sat down on the edge. But when she glanced up, several pretty girls in the nude were masquerading across the screen. A man holding leather whips was chasing them through a large field. Shen then turned away. Vulgarity was nothing she cared for. In fact, her embarrassment was more for Jeremy who, all of a sudden, seemed obsessed with pornography.

Words from the Bible then filtered through her mind. "If I regard iniquity in her heart, the Lord will not hear" (Psalms 66:18)

Minutes later she was able to slip quietly from the room, unseen. But at last glance, Jeremy's eyes were still glued to the television screen.

***

A few days later, after unlocking the back door, Hannah stepped inside and dropped her keys on the counter. "You're home early," she said, surprised because Jeremy's car wasn't in its usual place. Matthew then climbed from her arms, dropped to the floor, and ran to the next room.

"Make me a sandwich," Jeremy said.

"We just came from school," she said. "Austin and Haley are right behind me." She then slipped her jacket off before tossing it on a chair. "I need a quick bathroom break, and I'll be right back."

"I said make me a sandwich," Jeremy said, his demand overriding her words."

"We just walked in the door. Please, give me a minute."

"I don't have a minute," he said, but his voice was more of a growl. "I'm playing golf with that new minister this afternoon." His fist then pounded the table. "I'm in a hurry. Where's my clubs?"

But the scowl on his face was disturbing, so Hannah quickly pushed the children down the hall, and into a bedroom. "Where you left them," she said, upon her return. Still shaking, she lifted a loaf of bread.

"I said, fix me a sandwich," he yelled. He then reached down, and grabbed a large piece of splintered firewood from a metal container adjacent to the wood stove. The next instant the projectile grazed past her head as it jetted through the air.

Her hair fluttered in the draft before a colossal thud exploded in the room. Haley rounded the corner just seconds before a second piece propelled toward Hannah. She bolted when he reached for another.

But when the last slab plunged through the air, it grazed past Hannah's head before crashing into the attached clock on the cook stove. Then, as pieces of shattered glass littered the appliance, she touched her head, expecting blood.

"Thank God he missed," she whispered. And immediately a Bible verse popped into her head. "You intended to harm me, but God intended it for good to accomplish what is now being done, the saving of many lives" (Genesis 50:20)

Later that week Haley returned home with a stack of school papers tucked away in her satchel. But while thumbing through the pile later that evening, Hannah noticed one circled in red. Haley's account of the firewood incident had been marked by her first grade teacher.

***

Several days later, after things had somewhat settled, it was again time to fall in line with Jeremy's guidelines. Coats were donned, the door opened and three hesitant children then ambled past.

Minutes earlier, severe pain had flooded Hannah's head, as cluster migraines overtook her senses. But without success she tried to ease the throbs and reduce the maze of geometric designs light sensitivity created. She was also nauseous. Still, it didn't matter. Barely able to see one step in front of the other, yet she realized compliance to Jeremy's demand was her only recourse. An hour of driving lay ahead. Could I make it?

The children, now headed to the car, were in front of her. The next instant she stumbled, and missed a step on her descent from the porch. But her arm caught the rail just before she would have tumbled to the ground, and she was able to steady herself. "Thank God, I'm okay," she whispered.

Cold rain, now a steady downpour, pelted the ground as she staggered to the car. But once inside she turned the wipers on, slid the seatbelt over her chest, and felt around for the switch.

"Haley, make sure your brothers are strapped in," she said. Barely able to see for herself, Hannah would need her assistance during the trip.

"Okay, Mama," Haley said.

Still blinded by the migraine, Hannah could only pray God would steer the car for them.

"Haley, please close the car door."

"Do we have to go, Mama," Austin asked.

"Your father insisted we drive up for the church picnic," Hannah said. "He said we had to be there."

"It takes forever to get to church anyway," Haley said; then pulled out a game, opened it, and passed out player pieces to her siblings.

The key was then inserted, the car sputtered, and purred from the curb. But seeing through the window was all but impossible, so Hannah twisted around; trying to find a more comfortable way to drive.

"If I didn't know better, I'd say this picnic has been cancelled," she said.

The next instant Austin smacked his sister on the back on the arm. "Mama, make Austin stop," Haley whined

"Hey guys," Hannah said, rubbing her head, and squinting. "I'm having a hard time driving through this rain. I've got a terrible headache, and I need some peace and quiet on this trip. Please, work with me now."

She then turned the car onto the main road, praying for God's mercy; all the while realizing Jeremy's wallops would be applied if they didn't show up. "Oh, God. My head hurts so much. It's killing me," she said under her breath. "But why do I have these migraines?" Again she squinted, trying to see the road.

The next instant a squirrel scooted across the lane, and the brakes slammed. "Oh, God, please help me—help us," Hannah said. *I've probably been hit in the head too many times. I should be home, and in bed.*

Again the car rolled on, but she continued rubbing her head. Often, when a migraine hit, she would stagger when walking. *But what if this is caused by another medical issue? Jeremy refuses doctor visits. He says I'm fine, even when my head throbs.*

"I hope it stop raining," Haley said, interrupting her thoughts. "This picnic won't be any fun if it keeps raining."

"I know, honey. But, it doesn't matter. We still have to be there."

"Why does Daddy make you go when you have a headache?" Austin asked. "I get to stay home when I'm sick."

"I don't know," Hannah said, and a long sigh escaped. "But all of you need to stay as quiet as you can. I need to concentrate on the road. Between the rain and my blurry eyes, I can barely see a thing."

Still she continued to drive, squinting through the headache daze as the slickened roadway raced around her eyes. *If I don't drive faster, we'll lose time. But if I drive slower, we'll be late.*

Again she blinked. The car light coming at them was blinding, and she swerved to keep from hitting the driver. After that, as a precaution, her acceleration slowed dramatically.

Oh, God—help us. Please be with us. Please keep us safe. But why is it necessary to always do exactly what Jeremy says? Well, I know. He'll beat me up if I don't.

***

Later, after several harrowing episodes, the car rolled into the church parking lot; unscathed. Again blinking tears away, Hannah stumbled from the car; still thanking God for their safety.

I don't know how we made it on our own. God must have been watching over us, or we wouldn't be here now.

Chapter Eighteen

Weathering the Storm

Years of assaults and untold battery had Hannah worn down to the point she no longer cared for herself. Only the children kept her focused, and helped her to stay strong.

Bruises and black eyes were normal for her on any given day. But if Jeremy's family didn't care, and the church didn't notice, then life would continue without recourse. And yet she realized this type of mistreatment couldn't be right. Although he sometimes apologized, on the inside she felt unimportant, and wasted.

Everyday conflicts were getting harder to understand. Because when his actions fell short, her accountability soared—finding his lost keys, accepting blame for his running late, to even what he wore. His wants and desires always overrode her needs. Compliance, however, was essential for maintaining the peace.

Still she wished there was someone she could talk to who would realize her crisis, and tell her what to do. But no one seemed interested. So, after many prayers and untold deliberation, she decided to record Jeremy's rants as no one would acknowledge he was an abuser. One day she might need proof.

The following evening, when he came through the door, Hannah grabbed the recorder, switched it on, and quickly shoved it behind a towel.

"What do you think you're doing?" he asked, and then strode toward her. *He saw me. What do I do now?*

The next instant he jerked the machine from its

hiding place, and hurled it against the wall. But as shattered pieces of plastic and metal littered the floor, he stepped even closer.

"Just what are you trying to record?" he asked, and lunged at her. "Now clean this mess up, and don't ever record me again."

A fist then plunged her shoulder, lifted, and came at her face. Yet dodging his arm was futile, and she landed hard against the door; where a foot kicked her in the shins.

"You'd better not buy another recorder," he said. "If you do, I'll kill you."

Cold tiles reached up to meet Hannah when a fist slammed her face. Then, as blood dripped from her mouth, her eye began to swell. But he only laughed, stepped over her legs, and walked away.

***

Shaken, and still terrified, Hannah decided to report the assault to the police. But calling this time them felt safe as Jeremy was visiting Emily at her home, two doors down. Yet, because of that call, action outside the window was now holding her attention. Police cars were parking at Emily's house, and Hannah drew a quick breath.

"They're here," she whispered out loud. "At least this time they responded." But then her heart began to pound. She took a deep breath, grabbed her jacket, and then rushed outside. Two policemen in blue uniform were staring at her from the steps of Emily's porch as she hurried down the street.

"At least they responded," she whispered again, then prepared to join the group. "Maybe they'll do something this time."

But as she stepped closer, she noticed Mark, Ashley's husband, sitting on a wide porch swing; lazily swaying back and forth in the gentle breeze. His wavy brown hair wafted in the breeze, and he looked as unconcerned as the smile on his face. Still, she could only speculate why he was at Emily's house, and not at work.

Then she glanced at Jeremy, who was calmly leaning against a porch rail; quite relaxed, and unafraid. Emily, face unreadable, stood silently in the doorway, and stared at her. But when she reached the group, Mark turned and pointed his finger directly at her.

"She's the crazy one," he said.

Startled, Hannah stopped midway up the steps. This wasn't what she had expected. Acute fear then gripped her by the throat as she recalled the last time the police were alerted, but no one responded. Later, when asked, the officer's response had been chilling. "We know your husband," he had said. "He would never assault anyone."

The next instant she jolted back. One of the officers was speaking.

"You need psychiatric help, lady," he said. "Can you justify your report?" And instantly her legs grew weak.

Again she glanced at Jeremy, then took a deep breath. "He punched me in the face and shoulders," she said, and then fidgeted with her finger while waiting for a response.

"You look fine to me." The officer was scoffing. "I don't see any evidence of violence."

Jeremy's face then revealed a look of achievement, as if taunting her. But since there was no recourse, Hannah turned away; and stumbled back down the road.

"The police didn't believe me after all," she whispered. "What else could I do but leave?"

Her face flamed as the truth of her reality was again swept under the rug. She was still on her own. Did she know even one person who would stand with her?

Her heart continued to pound as both frustration and disbelief flooded her mind.

"So do not be afraid of them. There is nothing concealed that will not be disclosed, or hidden that will not be made known" (Matthew 10:26)

There wasn't any doubt another beating was in Hannah's future.

***

The following week Mrs. Allen stopped by, prepared to watch the children for the afternoon. "The kids will be fine while you're gone," she said as she sat down on a porch chair. She dropped her purse on the concrete step, waved at the Haley and Austin in the sand box, and then asked, "Who's cutting your hair?"

"That new place in town," Hannah said. "I forgot the name."

"The one Emily told you about?"

"Yes, that's the one."

"Will you stop and pick me up a loaf of bread on the way home?"

"I'll be glad to," Hannah said, then handed a toy to the baby.

"We're not going anywhere," Mrs. Allen said, and tousled her grandson's hair. "We'll be just fine playing in the sand, won't we honey?"

"I promise I won't be gone long," Hannah said; then grabbed her purse, kissed Matthew again, and waved at the other two in the sandbox.

"Take your time," Mrs. Allen said.

"Thanks for helping me out."

"We'll wash my car in a little bit," she said. "We'll stay busy."

"Bye for now," Hannah said, then hurried to the car. It was nice having a little time to herself.

"Your last name sounds familiar," the stylist said. "Are you related to that preacher who works at Tyler's Furniture?"

"You mean Jeremy?" And instantly Hannah sucked in her breath. "Yes. That's the one," she said.

Now uneasy with the questions, she shifted in the chair. "He's my husband." *This is so embarrassing. I didn't know she knew him.*

"Really?" The stylist then stopped the trim, swirled the chair again, and again pumped it higher.

"Yes, really," Hannah said, and tried to conceal her red face.

"You know, I've heard so many good things about him," she said.

How I wish I was somewhere else. I want to run away. If I could, I would.

"He's very good looking," she said, continuing her banter. "Dresses fine. Nice man—friendly too."

"Thanks."

"You don't know how lucky you are having him for a husband."

Silence.

Although Hannah glanced up, she said nothing. Any response would have been inappropriate. It was obvious this lady didn't have a clue.

Chapter Nineteen

Threats

Once home Hannah grabbed her grocery bag, and scrambled from the car. But she instantly stopped after noting several heads bobbing through the bay window. She then slowed her pace to a crawl, opened the back door, and squeezed inside. She could only pray no one would see her.

Stealth was a recent technique she now used to gather information as her own advocate. Playing detective was serious business after she learned a cheating husband was the reason her life was more brutal than before.

But why were members of Jeremy's family at her house? And why was he home? Was this a private family meeting she wasn't invited to? Or, perhaps, they were here to rally for her.

She cautiously stepped into hearing distance, but then stopped dead in her tracks. Jeremy's voice, loud and clear, was blasting from a few feet away.

"If she doesn't stay out of my business," he said, "I swear I'll blow her brains out."

His words were revealing. Was he talking about her? Well, probably. Recent actions indicated his hatred was growing. She could only imagine his intent.

Robert, another brother-in-law, piped up. "You don't want to do that," he said.

What was he doing here?

Emily's voice then cut in. "Now calm down, Jeremy," she said. "No need to even think about killing her. If you can't work things out, there's always the option of getting divorced."

"She's been nosing around," he said. "She just needs to stay out of her life."

Mrs. Allen's voice then conveyed words of calm dispute. "What about the children? You don't want to repeat your father."

"I don't want to hear it," he said.

"Then don't be like him."

"You don't understand," he said. And his voice sounded rough, and intentionally harsh. The next instant a loud thud penetrated the wall.

That's probably him hitting something with his fist.

"If she gets in my way, I promise I'll blow her brains out."

"That's crazy," Rick said. "You don't know what you're saying, man."

But Hannah knew exactly why Jeremy was angry. When driving past his work earlier that week, she had noticed a woman she didn't know having what appeared to be an intimate conversation with him. And the way he responded every time the phone rang was also noted. He would take off in his car like a mad man. Probably meeting someone—probably pre-planned too.

It was impossible to count the times he'd left the house after the phone rang. But when asked, he would threaten to kill her. Not to mention the time she stopped by a convenience store with the children, and he was there. No problem cursing her out—and in front of the children too.

"I'll blow your brains out," were Jeremy's favored words. And yet Hannah had never taken him seriously. Maybe now she should.

What about that earring she had found? Who did that belong to?

A blue, diamond shaped earring had been discovered in the floorboard of the car after the door opened. But when questioned, Jeremy had become angry, and insolent.

"Are you having an affair?" her words were scripted.

"What do you think?" Jeremy's words were acid,

although his eyelid twitched, and he looked somewhat irritated.

"I think you are."

"That's none of your business," he said,

"Then you are having an affair," Hannah said, and her heartbeat accelerated.

"No, I'm not. Are you?" Again his words were insulting.

"I'm not the one missing an earring."

"I don't know where it came from," he said, and then walked to the door.

"Well, you know it isn't mine. I don't wear earrings."

Reeling around, he gaited back, grabbed the earring, and shoved it in his pocket.

"Why did you—?"

"None of your business."

"I think it is."

"Shut up, bitch," he said. "Just leave me alone." He then turned, grabbed his keys, and slammed the door on his way out. Seconds later the car cranked, and he was gone—again.

What about the time he was parked on the side of the road? Was he waiting to meet someone?

"What are you doing here?" he asked, when she stopped. But he had waved her away—words of profanity streaming from his mouth.

Terror then grabbed Hannah senses. His look was more than frightening, and she dreaded even the thought of later going home. Still, clues of his rendezvous kept showing up—right in her face. All she had to do was watch for them. There was no way she could trust him now. And he wanted to blow her brains out?

Yet she didn't have time to worry. Between him and three kids, she was busy twenty-four seven. Still she wanted him to know she was aware of his misdeeds. But was he? And would his family believe, after hearing his threats in person?

How many times had she mentioned her plight, and

they simply blew it off? "Maybe he'll change." Everyone said it. Were those words of concern, or just denial?

"Words are all I'll ever get from his family," Hannah whispered softly.

Still she couldn't understand Jeremy's hatred. What had she ever done to deserve such contempt? And did he really intend to kill her? What about the kids? Didn't he care about them?

Her mind was again playing tricks—forcing hurtful thoughts to engulf her sanity.

***

That same evening Mrs. Allen decided to stay the night, and sleep on the sofa. Her plan—to see if her son acted out.

Later, after Jeremy went to the bedroom, a thunderous clatter erupted. And instantly Hannah ran to the room. He was dumping her personal items in a trash can.

"Please don't throw my perfume away," she said, begging. Her favorite outfit was now in pieces. An opened pair of scissors lay on the bed beside them. The next instant a raw fist belted her in the face, then came at her shoulder. And instantly she dropped to the floor, writhing in pain.

"You're such a bitch," he said; his words callous and degrading. Yet when she dared to stand, he again shoved her down.

"Don't move," he said. "Don't you dare move."

More than fearful, Hannah cringed, and then drew into herself. Terrified, she remained in her place, afraid to move.

***

A few minutes later, after Jeremy sat down on the bed, Hannah was able to stand. But she leaned against the wall for support, hoping he wouldn't notice. Her eye was now swelling, and her vision disrupted. Concerned, she reached up, and touched the puffy lid. But the way it felt, she knew it was also turning black.

Her legs felt wobbly. In fact, her entire body was weak. Yet he didn't care. He just flopped on the bed and howled with laughter.

Still frightened, she struggled with the outcome; hoping Mrs. Allen would come to her rescue. But after realizing she wasn't, she managed to slip away from Jeremy, and then edge from the room. Still the coarseness of hilarity followed as she stumbled back down the hall.

But when she reached the living room, Mrs. Allen glanced up from where she sat on the edge of the sofa, waiting.

"He just hit me," Hannah said, again holding her shattered jaw, and limping.

"I don't know that he hit you," Mrs. Allen said.

"Well, he just did."

"I don't know that he did," she said. "I didn't see him do it."

Chapter Twenty

Tennis Partner

"I'm taking the day off," Jeremy said, opening the closet door. Then, with a look of arrogance, he tucked a colorful shirt into a new pair of white shorts, pulled a thin tennis sweater from the opening, and casually slung it over his shoulder.

Hannah couldn't help but giggle as he strutted through the house, admiring his new attire. Still he wasn't easily forthcoming, and she wondered what he was really up to. But, she was suspicious.

"I'll be gone all morning," he said, then grabbed his keys off the counter. He swiveled to the door, stopped, and then glanced around for another glimpse of his back side.

"Where are you going?" Hannah asked.

"None of your business," he shot back.

"It is my business," she said, following close behind.

"Not really," he said, but continued his stride to the car. "I'm playing tennis, if you must know."

Stepping closer, she asked, "What tennis court?"

"You know which one," he said, then rolled the window half-way down after slamming the door. "You'd better not follow me either, if you know what's good for you."

"What do you mean?"

"I said you'd better not follow me if you know what's good for you."

"What—"

"If you come where I'm playing tennis, I'll kill you." His jaw was set; and yet his actions didn't surprise her. His hateful attitude was what she now expected from him.

She walked back to the house as the sound of his revved-up engine roared in her ear. Turning, she glimpsed the tail end of his red sedan as it rounded the corner, and disappeared. In the distance the motor accelerated as his car sped through town.

In the past Hannah always said a prayer for Jeremy's safety. But now, after all she had been through, she couldn't honestly pray those words. She no longer wanted him back.

On the other hand, her curiosity was getting the best of me. Maybe she would play detective again, and take the kids for a short ride. It was time to learn what he was really up to.

An hour later Hannah and the children jumped in the car, and drove to the designated tennis court. In the distance a woman much younger than she flagged a racket back and forth as she swiveled toward a yellow tennis ball. Her skirt bared slim legs to the hip, and whipped about in the gentle breeze. But, again, Hannah wasn't surprised. In fact, she had expected as much.

She parked, cut the engine, and then stared out the car window; arms crossed. Minutes later Jeremy glanced in their direction, turned, and barged toward the car. His already reddened cheeks flamed, and he wiped a sweaty residue from his brow.

Fear again engulfed Hannah on the inside, and she took a ragged breath—preparing for the onslaught coming at her. Her boldness would certainly cost her. Still she didn't regret seeing Jeremy's tennis partner for herself. At least she deserved that much.

"You piece of shit," he said, and then spit more vulgar, derogating words through clinched teeth. "I warned you not to come here."

Again she drew a staggered breath, but remained silent; trying to stay calm.

"Get these kids out of here," he said, and pointed at their three gazing out the car window. His next words were barked. "Don't ever come back here, bitch. I'll kill you if you do."

Killing must certainly be on Jeremy's mind. He was tormenting Hannah with those words—almost on a daily basis. The next instant he spun on his heel, turned, and marched back to the tennis court where he and his partner again twisted and swayed to the beat of tennis rackets.

Hannah let out a long sigh. Then, as her car headed out, her head began to droop. The reality of her investigation was now sinking in, and she wiped a tear away. Jeremy was openly betraying their marriage vows without a second thought.

***

Later that same evening Jeremy's foul mouth and arrogant mood only excelled.

"You're just a piece of trash," he shouted after his return home. Still angry, he strode forward; and from his lips jetted a stream of spit that splashed Hannah in the face. The next instant she was sprawled on the floor.

"Who gave you permission to come by the tennis court, and see me?" he asked.

"No—no one."

"Don't you ever follow me—not ever again."

Then, as her tongue tasted a warm substance, she licked her lips, and again reached up. Splotches of sticky red remained on the tips of her fingers.

"You know what else?" he asked—breath hot on her neck. "I've been with lots of women, and they're all better than you."

How can he say that to me? More women than his tennis partner?

He stood, arms folded, and stared down. "Got a problem?"

Still cowering, Hannah pulled herself up; but remained frightened.

"I can treat you any way I want, and you can't do one thing about it" Jeremy said, and his torso whipped back and forth as if mocking her. "What do you have to say about that?"

"I don't know," she said, still cowering.

The next instant his hand formed a fist, as if ready to pelt her again.

"Please don't," she said, glancing up, then down again.

"You know why I'm not worried?" he asked, words purring as they mocked.

The word "No," quietly slipped from her lips.

"Because we're married, and we'll always be married."

Yet she remained silent. His look was toxic, and she instinctively recoiled. *All I ever wanted was a loving husband. And now, what do I have?*

"I can treat you any way I want," he said again, and his lips curled. "You'll never leave me."

It was best if Hannah remained silent. Jeremy's anger could easily leave her in a heap of disfigurement. He was in his blame game again. She would just ride it out until he calmed down. After years of practice, she knew staying quiet worked best when he played his mind games. So she clamped her lips, and wrapped her arms around her chest—just in case.

***

"Someone at work cashed in their retirement," Jeremy said two days later. "I think I'll do the same."

One brief moment Hannah stopped washing the dishes—somewhat interested, but not much. "Why?" she asked. Still her words were guarded.

"So we can get out of debt," he said. And, for the first time in a long time, he sounded pleased.

"How much money?"

"A few thousand."

The thought of being debt-free then whirred through her mind. Since his resignation as church pastor, Jeremy was now employed full-time at Tyler Furniture. Still, money was hard come by, and an added stress for her. But she was thankful his masquerade as church pastor had ended some time before.

Perhaps after things were paid off, she could leave the marriage debt free. By now she was more than ready. Deceived, betrayed, and battered; yet the claws of abuse still held her deep within its guttural clutch. But perhaps—and a small flicker of hope stirred in her heart.

"We'll pay everything off, and split what's left—fifty-fifty," Jeremy said; then picked up a pencil, and began tapping the table top. "Get me some paper."

Hannah grabbed a notepad and handed it to him.

"What all do we owe?" he asked, and the tapping stopped. "Let's make a list."

Their debt was then quoted from memory. But after jotting down some numbers, he started rummaging through a kitchen drawer. "Where's the calculator?" he asked.

"In the desk—over here," she said, then lifted the instrument and handed it to him. Still, the sound of fingers tapping keys was encouraging.

"This should be enough to pay off our credit cards, one car, and the appliances," he said.

"Are you sure cashing in your retirement is what you want to do?"

"Everybody's doing it," he said, and then the tapping stopped. "Besides, it's an easy way out of debt."

"I'm not so sure."

It was, after all, his money. He should be the one to decide how it was spent. Always, when decisions were questioned, he got mad. So, for now, trusting his opinion was best. But keeping things in perspective would keep alive the suspicion he might change his mind. And since he was openly fooling around, what were his true intentions?

He stood, and then abruptly sat back down. "It only takes a couple of weeks to get the money," he said.

"Really?"

But, for now, Hannah refused to get excited. Jeremy's ideas always kept her too stressed to think beyond the moment. Already a lifetime of hopes had been crushed.

It was hard seeing beyond a crisis, so she clutched at the thought of a brighter day, and tried to believe a better future could exist, but far in the distance.

Yet Jeremy's subdued manner was somewhat confusing, so Hannah decided to simply stay out of his way. Did he have a change of heart? Was he repentant? She could only pray it was so.

Chapter Twenty-One

Christmas Fiasco

Christmas was just around the corner, and yet Hannah dreaded the season. Over the years she had learned to squelch her feelings; realizing it was best to remain complacent, and detached. Even the thought of a holiday was challenging.

Nothing ever changed in the scheme of things although, after several battering episodes, her physical appearance was somewhat questionable. Not only was she exhausted, but also depressed. For her, the joy of the season was dead. Looking the part of a happy wife was tiring as her heart was more than broken.

What did her marriage offer that was worth preserving? She had husband who no longer strove to be a Christian, much less a minister of the gospel? His roving eye captured the attention of women, and he gleefully flaunted his excursions in her face without batting an eye. But his attempt to disguise the deception hadn't mislead Hannah at all. It was easy, after a few investigative measures, to uncover his secrets.

Hannah dressed in silence for Jeremy's company party, overcome with the pressure of the unknown. Nervous reservations had again surfaced. The invitation, a personal request from his female employer, was insulting. However, he was excited over the upcoming festivity, and insisted she attend with him. But she dreaded the ruse, and desired to stay home. He was adamant, however, so she prepared for the party, and prayed she could endure the evening.

Would anyone at the party be aware that Jeremy and the hostess had been seen together at a local motel? If the gossip was true, how should she react? Secretly she wondered how the charade would play out. Maybe she could catch him in his own lies. The children would be staying with Grams—one less worry on her mind.

***

Later, as Hannah and Jeremy climbed the short steps of a nice brick home, her heart skipped a beat. Was she dressed well enough? It was doubtful as her wardrobe was limited. And immediately she felt out of place when a sparkling lady in evening attire opened the door. And who wouldn't be swayed by someone this dazzling?

Later, as the evening progressed, Hannah found herself sitting on a sofa with the woman's husband, whose breath reeked of alcohol. He was non-talkative, and consumed glass after glass of liquor without batting an eye. His initial beverage offer had been declined. Instead she sipped a wine glass full of sprite, and remained a silent observer. But what was the man trying to cover up? And why would anyone drink so heavily?

After a time she noticed Jeremy and the hostess together, sitting in a cozy nook. But as she scrutinized the couple, they leaned into each other, deep in conversation. How easily this had happened. Still she couldn't keep her eyes off the two. His glass had been re-filled several times. Was he also getting plastered?

Boredom, disgust, and disappointment now held Hannah bound. Would this evening never end? She would rather be at home than a partner to this weird fiasco.

***

Later, sometime after midnight, Jeremy staggered off the front steps, and into the yard. And, as usual, Hannah followed close behind. But when his silly, high-pitched laughter echoed through the courtyard, she turned red, and sighed with embarrassment. The next instant he reeled, and faced the hostess.

"It's been funny," he said. "Thanks for the inanition."

Was he drunk? Never before had Hannah seen Jeremy this way. But as she stood waiting, he began to throw up in the yard. His face turned pale, and he now stunk of alcohol and vomit.

How much more disgusting could he get? How much more degrading can this be?

Hannah reached inside her purse, and searched for a set of car keys. "I'm driving," she said, and waved them in the air.

But instead of arguing with her, Jeremy complied without hesitation; although he staggered on his way to the passenger side of the car.

"I knew I'd need a driver," he said, a giggle in his throat. "That's the only reason I brought you along." His words were also slurred.

God help me.

But once home, Hannah parked the car, helped Jeremy inside, and into bed; thankful the evening was finally over. For once his true character as liar, cheat, and drunkard had been exposed. This wasn't the preacher man she had married. This was a complete stranger.

***

Three days later Jeremy sauntered into the kitchen holding Haley by the hand. "I'm leaving for a while," he said. "And, I'm taking her with me."

Jeremy never took the kids anywhere. Where was he going this time?

Hannah reached for Haley, but ducked when he took a swat at her. And instantly she bristled as deep fear engulfed her mind.

"No, please don't take her," she said, hands

outstretched

"Shut up," he said, and his eyebrows lifted in a menacing way. Still, the sound of his voice was strong, and Hannah cowered in uncertainty and dread.

He then shoved her aside, and stepped outside. He hoisted Haley to his shoulders, walked to the car, and they both climbed in. And immediately they were gone.

But where was he taking Haley this late in the afternoon? Hannah's hands shook uncontrollably as fear again overcame her senses.

***

The face on the clock registered ten-thirty eight as darkness engulfed the outside—just as fear engulfed Hannah's heart. The next instant the door opened, and she leaped from the sofa. She ran to the kitchen just as Jeremy stepped inside. Haley was asleep in his arms.

Overcome with emotion, Hannah released a huge sigh of relief. She then shook herself free of restless anxieties, and followed Jeremy to Haley's bedroom. But once there she stood in silence as he placed Haley on the bed, using more care than ever before seen from him. Then, without saying one word, he headed to the living room. And instantly television voices flooded the air.

Hannah tucked Haley under the cover, grateful she was again safe at home.

The following day Haley provided details of visiting a pretty lady's house where she was given candy and ice-cream. A red balloon drifting through the living-room had been another gift from the same woman. Still, Hannah could only speculate who the mystery lady was, but supposed it was Jeremy's female boss. Yet she dared not say a word. Fear of the unknown then flooded her mind as she realized her life was now in more danger than ever before.

***

A few days following the party and Jeremy again threatened to kill Hannah. But at this point she was afraid of her own shadow, and feared retaliation if she tried to defend herself.

When would it end? And did she dare learn more about the darker side of her husband's life? Although abused, lied to, and cheated on, she still desired the missing elements of a concrete marriage—love, respect, and trust.

While growing up, she never once saw a man hit a woman. But in her own marriage, the necessity of hiding secrets while masquerading under the guise of happiness was essential. Was she too sheltered as a child to understand that a bad marriage could exist? She had lived a secluded life on a farm, protected from the world outside by hard labor, few necessities, and even fewer friends.

Lacking a social network she could now trust was a huge disadvantage as her only associates were Jeremy's family, and the people she attended church with. But they remained uninterested, or unaware she was a battered woman. And so she withdrew even further, and continued to live in silence.

Chapter Twenty-Two

Stolen Sanity

The sun dipped behind the horizon as Hannah sat—alone—perched on an outside porch step with her head bent over. The children were asleep, allowing time to think of ways to escape her broken marriage. Whatever it took, she was now game. Life was getting more dangerous with each passing day. But mostly, the children needed a more peaceful home life.

"He causes His sun to rise on the evil and the good, and sends rain on the righteous and the unrighteous" (Matthew 5:45)

"Thank you, Jesus, for reminding me of this verse."

She pulled her coat close, and an inner strength surged. She now realized this was the perfect time to seriously plan her getaway. But when should she leave? And how? No, she couldn't just leave. She would need to escape. *God, please help me. I need your help.*

"Where are you?"

Her body twitched in response to Jeremy's insistent tone, and a weathered flowerpot tilted and spilled; sending dry dirt and a dead geranium tumbling down the porch steps. An overwhelming fear then gripped her by the throat. Last evening's assault was still fresh in her mind, and she was instantly conflicted on how to respond.

The next instant he turned, and flopped down on a nearby chair. Disgraceful terms demeaning her very existence began to tumble nonstop from his lips, and she cowered beneath his gaze. *What will he now do?*

He wasn't drunk as most would expect from someone so verbal. For the most part he didn't. Still admired and respected all over town as a minister of the gospel, he maintained a solid and irreproachable label. No one dared think less of him than who he portrayed himself to be.

He's called me these same names many times. Later he'll say he's sorry, and that would be the end of it—as far as he's concerned. Was this what my dad meant when he said, "You've made your bed, now sleep in it?"

The evening shadows around them seemed indifferent to Jeremy's arrogant laughter as they sifted in the gentle breeze. But, for Hannah, the sound was pure evil.

"If you're thinking about leaving me, well—don't even think about it," he said. His words, spoken through gritted teeth, pierced her heart; and she bristled.

How could he possibly know I was planning to leave him?

Nearby the crickets chirped an evening croon as the day's lingering warmth closed in around them. Jeremy's next words instantly jerked her back.

"If you leave, I'm keeping the kids."

Her hands began to quiver, and she sucked in her breath. Dread then summoned a nightmare of emotions. What more could he say?

"Don't even think about taking them away from me," he said. His words were laced with profanity.

I'm not a lying whore.

"You'll never take her kids from me."

You don't care about your kids.

"If you do, I'll kidnap them back, and you'll never see them again."

His words were strong, and again slapped Hannah in the face. But out of habit, she recoiled; and withdrew even further into herself. The next instant waves of terror ripped through her torso, and her heart pulsated wildly as it exploded into her extremities. *Could he really keep the kids if I left him? And would he?*

The twilight's fading tranquility failed to ignite a

sense of harmony inside her despairing soul.

"You won't get anything in the house either, you ugly bitch. Don't even try." His teeth were still gritted.

Was he serious, or just playing another mind game? And would a judge let him to keep the kids if they went to court?

Hannah's twisted hands were now drenched, and her forehead furrowed, in response to Jeremy's temperament. Instead of responding, she became a coward—afraid to speak, or to even defend herself.

"I'll kill you before I let you have my kids," he said. His words, sharp and to the point, cut like a knife.

Still she sat, rigid and stiff on the step, as dreams of a blissful life began to slowly dissolve—dreams of escaping her abuser—dreams of keeping the children safe from harm.

Her cold hands then oozed a sweaty residue, and she firmly gripped them together. But the imprint of nails was jagged and painful as they dug deep into her palms.

An old adage then came to mind. *Hold your hands and you will remain calm, and relaxed.* She squeezed them again, but tighter this time, and prayed those words were true.

"Besides, everybody thinks you're the one with the problem."

His words again jarred her thoughts. But, he was right. No one believed he was a wife beater. Although every member in his family, at one time or another, had heard him say he was going to kill her, they instead chose to ignore the warning. Others believed he was a wonderful husband, and father.

New words, raw and twisted, again slammed her thoughts. More threats, mixed with vulgar oaths, rolled nonstop from his lips, and his fists beat together as if anticipating a brawl.

Yet, from experience, Hannah knew he intended to do exactly what he said. His words stung far worse than a fist ever had. *What does a snaggle-toothed whore look like anyway?*

Instant tears formed, and trickled down her cheek, but she quickly wiped them away. She dared not allow him the pleasure of her concern. What would he then do? Besides, if she showed fear, she was weak.

"He never before cared about the kids," she whispered. "Why now? And does he really intend to do everything he said? Or is he just saying those things to scare me?"

From instinct she stiffened, recalling many graphic injuries from the night before. Would tonight be the same? Could she endure more cruelty? And dare she risk his threats for her freedom?

He stood—silhouette tall and menacing in the moonlight. "Go ahead. Pack your bags and leave," he said. "But the kids aren't going with you."

No matter the circumstance, she would never leave without them. All she had, at this point, was God's word to keep her steady.

"...but those who hope in the LORD will renew their strength. They will soar on wings like eagles; they will run and not grow weary, they will walk and not be faint" (Isaiah 40:31)

If she didn't leave Jeremy soon, she was doomed. Without a doubt he would kill her, and the children wouldn't have a mother. He would then go to jail, and they would be raised by someone else.

Her refusal to give up would be a challenge. Yet, in her heart of hearts, Hannah felt that God would, somehow, see her through.

Fear then spurred her forward as words from the Bible filled her heart with hope. "Weeping may endure for a night, but joy comes in the morning" (Psalms 30:5)

Her insides churned as Jeremy's words again pelted her with even more chilling profanity. Did he have no remorse?

"God, strike me dead." Blasphemous words, spoken in anger, struck a new cord of horror in her heart. How could he say such things in front of God and man, and then preach in a church somewhere on Sunday?

She would never understand his logic. In fact, she had long ago stopped trying.

Chapter Twenty-Three

The Final Straw

Living on the edge had long been a pattern of accepted brutality, rage, and assault for Hannah. Jeremy's insensitivity made life a torturous nightmare. Routine battering and spiteful comments were now the norm on any given day. Yet today the children seemed oblivious to undercurrent problems in the home. They scooted about early Christmas morning playing with new toys and assorted gifts. *Thank God.*

Minutes later Jeremy sauntered to the room carrying an unwrapped attaché case. He leaned over, and then handed it Hannah. But his arrogance only brought instant tears to her eyes. Why would he give her a gift that someone, most likely, had purchased for him? She didn't need the case. What would she do with it?

Nothing was expected, or desired, from him. Recent assaults were too raw—too painful—too unforgettable. Yet, because his nature disallowed gift giving, his generosity was an undesired novelty. Her surprise, however, was an inadequate term for this unexpected bombshell. Instead, preparation for what was ahead kept her cautious, and focused.

Her recently obtained job was all part of a plan to leave the marriage. The emergency room was now first on her agenda after returning to work. Injuries from the week-end needed treatment, and documentation—also essential for the plan to work. But as far as Jeremy was concerned, her injuries were non-existent. His attitude illustrated he simply wanted them to disappear.

Well, this time they wouldn't. Hannah was determined to obtain documentation. She was also confident that the infidelity, assaults, and hatred would only increase if given the opportunity. Her one desire was to get her life back.

Later that afternoon, as she and Haley sat on the floor dressing Barbie's, Jeremy meandered to their corner, and stopped in front of them.

"Hey, you," he said, looking down. In his hand was the attaché. "I think I'll just keep this for myself," he said, and tapped the case with his fingers. "You don't deserve it."

***

A few days after Christmas Jeremy sat in his car racing the engine again and again as if a teenager. The next instant the engine sputtered, tires squealed, and he was out of range. His cashed-in retirement had just arrived in the mail. He scooped it up; promising to put the entire amount in the bank. Hannah could only pray he would.

Should she trust him, or ignore his actions? Every muscle in her body tensed as, once again, fear overtook her senses. What if he left town without giving her a dime?

In the back of her mind, plans to leave the marriage were escalating. Once school was out for the summer she would go. Less disruption for the children would make the transition easier to accomplish. Already, part of her paycheck from her new job had been stashed away.

With head bowed, and eyes closed, she prayed Jeremy would simply allow them to leave when the time came.

***

Later that same evening, as darkness closed in, harsh blows began to pound Hannah from all directions. The children, now asleep in their beds, were hopefully immune to the brutality that was occurring. But why was Jeremy mad? It was impossible to determine the reason

Hannah's body shook, and then quivered, as she ducked; trying to avoid the worst of his pummels.

Now frightened, she dropped to the floor in a fetal position, and covered herself as best she could. What else could she do? Should she run for help? Could she? And why was Jeremy angry? The minute he entered the room she felt his rage. Yet there was nothing she could do to dodge the hostility. Simply said, she was trapped.

But as a booted foot kicked her in the side, she recoiled on the floor; and ducked her head. She wrapped already swollen arms around her torso, and realized she was in for the beating of a lifetime. *Oh, God, help me. Am I going to die this time?*

An agonizing onslaught of kicks and punches, followed by harsh oaths, pelted her from all directions. *Who can help me? It's the middle of the night. All the neighbors are asleep.*

Again and again Jeremy's heavy boot hammered Hannah's stomach and thighs. Fresh blood then oozed from swollen lips after a rigid fist crushed her face. But his actions simply spoke his heart. *Oh God. Help me! Will I die right here on the floor? Will anybody know—or care?*

Minutes later, after a short respite, Jeremy turned and walked to the next room. Then, as soon as he was out of sight, Hannah stood on wobbly legs, staggered to the side door, and slipped through the opening.

But without looking back, she stumbled down the steps, and into the yard. Adrenalin propelled her forward as new strength ruptured her emotions.

"Help! Help! Somebody help me!"

A streetlight nearby cast eerie shadows on several cars parked out front, but the neighbor's houses remained dark, and hushed. No one came to the door. No light illuminated. And no one responded to her cry. The only sound in the obscure darkness was a dog barking in the distance. All was quiet—too quiet for a Friday night.

The next instant her body quivered as Jeremy grabbed her from behind. An onslaught of profanity then rolled from his guarded lips, making his toned down words even more sinister.

Should I struggle, or give in?

But as hair was jerked, and teeth cracked, she released a labored scream. His breath, now hot on her neck, indicated an out-of-control rage.

Strands of blooded curls floated to the ground as the burn of roughened asphalt ripped her feet to shreds. Her body, no longer hers, throbbed and blazed in the transit moonlight.

"Help! Help! Somebody help me!"

But instantly her voice was stifled. Yet she continued to struggle, realizing this could be her last chance to survive.

"Shut up. Shut up." Raw nails clawed soft flesh, digging new abrasions into already inflamed limbs. Her breathing, once heavy and labored, then became shallow as she fought for her very life. Breaking free was impossible.

Then, as exposed legs scraped uneven cement steps, she cried out in agony. But once inside the house, the tepid floor rose up to meet her when Jeremy dumped her from his arms. Her escape had failed.

Fresh profanity continued to roll from his lips as another punch caught her off guard. His feet were again engaged, and hammered her body with brute force. But the curses spewing from his mouth were words she would never utter, and certainly not who she was on the inside. His vulgarity was as crude and degrading as a discarded piece of trash.

Well, that's what he calls me—Trash.

"But, I'm not."

***

No longer could Hannah deny Jeremy's aggressive assaults coming against her. In fact, her very existence was based on restrictions and damaging outcomes. But could she somehow change the result?

Neglected and abused as a child, immaturity and ignorance reigned. Finding her place in society had also dwarfed as manipulation from emotional demons had created tremendous fear and confusion. Ignorance and wrong trust often forced blind mistakes.

Her children were now growing up in an unhealthy and dysfunctional environment. Already they had witnessed more mistreatment, manipulation, and exploitation than most.

Training received as a child restrained verbal or physical retaliation for Hannah. Emotional support from church and family had also delayed her escape, and reinforced the notion that deflecting Jeremy's assaults was futile. Still, in the back of her mind, she believed God's word would keep her grounded. He would be her solid rock, her shield, and her deliverer. His divine guidance would provide all the inner strength needed to hold firm her decision to leave her wasted marriage, and strike out on her own.

A perfect breakaway would fall into place when she ultimately stepped away. Of this she firmly believed because

"The LORD makes firm the steps of the one who delights in him; though he may stumble, he will not fall, for the LORD upholds him with His hand" (Psalms 37:23,24)

"The LORD is my light and my salvation; whom shall I fear? The LORD is the strength of my life; of whom shall I be afraid?" (Psalms 27:1)

Chapter Twenty-Four

End of the Beginning

The following day Jeremy pulled out his wallet, totally ignoring the ramifications of his assault on Hannah the previous night. "It's time to divide the retirement money I cashed in," he said.

He must be feeling guilty, or maybe—for once—he's keeping his word.

"All the outstanding debt is now paid" he said. He then reached out, and handed Hannah a handful of cash. "I promised we'd split what's left. You get two thousand, and I get two."

"Thanks," she said, and a sliver of a smile formed on swollen lips. Her words, although slow, were grateful, as she shoved several loose bills into her purse. *Thank you, God.*

***

"Come in," Hannah said, and her smile crooked as the ravages of abuse again took center stage.

"How did you get all those scrapes and black eyes?" Emily asked, after stepping through the door. "What happened?"

But Hannah only shrugged her shoulders. Jeremy was in the room.

"Well, you need a doctor," Emily said. "I'll take you."

"She doesn't need a doctor," Jeremy said, standing solid in the hallway

"I think she does."

"Well, she's not going to see one," he said, then turned away.

"She deserves what she gets," he said in dry undertones.

Emily stepped forward, and followed close behind Jeremy. "What did you just say?" she asked.

"Nothing—nothing you need to know about."

"Did you hit her?"

"Leave us alone," he said, turning around.

"She really needs a doctor," Emily said, then pointed at Hannah. "Just look at her."

"Don't you dare take her to the doctor," he said. "Just leave her alone. She's fine."

"I'll take you to the doctor," she said, looking Hannah in the eye. "Just say the word."

"Jeremy doesn't want you to," Hannah said, and her eyes darted away. "I'm okay, really. I only have a few bruises."

"Did he hit you?"

"Well—"

"You can go home now," Jeremy said, and waved his sister away. "She's fine."

Again she glanced at Hannah's bandages, and blackened eyes. "You need a doctor," she said.

Frightened, Hannah twisted the hem of her shirt. "I'll be okay," she managed to say.

Jeremy then turned, looked straight at Hannah, and raised an eyebrow. And, in response, she quickly lowered her head.

"She's not going to any doctor," he said, still frowning at his sister. "Just go on home."

Emily again looked at Hannah. "If you change your mind," she said, "just let me know."

All Hannah could do was to shrug, and then turn away.

Emily glanced at Jeremy one last time, then walked out the door.

But Hannah, as a way of compliance, turned, and

stumbled to the refrigerator. It was time to get lunch. *I can barely walk. I can hardly move. Oh, God, everything hurts—everything.*

She tried to suck up the pain, but it was impossible. "I've never hurt so much after a beating," she whispered. "But, he could have killed me. At least I'm still alive."

Jeremy, hovering nearby, refused to leave Hannah alone. He kept stepping in her way as if afraid she would try to leave. Still she ignored his actions as she shuffled around re-heating a pot of the kid's favorite soup. She wanted to stay clear of him. She still feared for her life.

Her keys had been stolen, her mobility removed, and her spirit crushed. What more could he do?

I'll just pretend everything's fine, and take care of the kids as normal. Nothing stops just because I'm injured.

***

Why don't you move in with me until Jeremy settles down?" Mrs. Allen asked after stopping by the house later that evening.

More than eager to get away, Hannah accepted her offer without a second thought.

Mrs. Allen turned, and then patted Jeremy on the shoulder. "Hannah's going home with me for a couple of days," she said, "and the kids."

Clothes were then packed, under Jeremy's direction. And, minutes later, Hannah and the children were driving away from the house. For once he agreed they needed time apart.

***

Monday arrived, and not soon enough, as far as Hannah was concerned. Mrs. Allen's breakfast was then devoured, but jumbled nerves had kept her from eating. The kids, on the other hand, grabbed at the bacon with eager fingers. At least they weren't worried. And, for that, she was thankful.

106

"I'll get dressed," she said, again glancing at the clock.

Still thinking ahead, Hannah tried to visualize her day. A loose-fitting skirt would look best for hiding limps. Flat shoes would also benefit if she stumbled while climbing stairs. And, thank God for make-up. Her secret stash always seemed to come in handy. But when applied, she turned and stared hard in the mirror. Staring back was a drained, battered, and scared looking woman.

But as three-year-old Matthew ran past, joy flooded her injured soul. In fact, he was one of the reasons she was still standing.

"What are you and Grams doing today?" she asked, giving him a squeeze.

"Watching Pooh," he said, then blew her a kiss before racing to the next room.

Minutes later she was driving Haley and Austin to school.

***

Hoping no one would notice, Hannah slipped into her office, and closed the door. She propped her leg on a stool beneath the desk, and then prayed her unkempt appearance would remain hidden. And so began the day.

But when the clock struck noon, she again slipped down the stairs; all the while praying no one would notice. However, a couple of salesman saw her, and broke the silence.

"What's going on?" one asked. "You look like you've been knocked around the block."

At first she started to cover for Jeremy, as usual. But she then decided it best to reveal the ruse.

"My husband beat me up this past week-end," she said, and lowered her head.

"What a jerk. Anything I can do?"

"If Jeremy comes around, please—please don't let him come upstairs to my office."

"Don't worry," he said, and his smile was encouraging. "He won't come anywhere near you. I promise."

She tried to smile before saying good-bye, then limped her way to the parking lot. But in the background, endearing words floated back to her ears. "She's too nice to be treated that way."

"I'll whip his you-know-what if he shows up around here again," the other said. Although course, their words brought a warming sensation to Hannah's troubled mind. Maybe someone was watching over her after all.

***

Minutes later, as Hannah drove through the hospital entrance, she maintained her commitment, and parked the car before stumbling out. At the entrance, two revolving doors opened into a wide expanse of waiting rooms, and she staggered through them. But at the far end of the room she noticed a receptionist standing at a huge desk.

"May I help you?" the lady asked as Hannah moved closer.

"My husband beat me up this past week-end," she said, then rubbed her sweaty palms together. "Actually, twice in eight days."

"Do you need a doctor?"

"Yes, please."

"Wait here," the receptionist said.

Minutes later, a male nurse was escorting Hannah into an enclosed examining room. The curtains were then drawn, and she was left alone to re-think her decision of sitting on a cold gurney in the middle of the day.

Later, in what seemed like hours, a doctor was examining her injuries. X-rays followed.

"You have several fractured ribs," he said. "Here. Look at this." And he pointed at several bone fractures highlighted on the screen. "We use large elastic bands for injuries like this. It helps to ease the pain while the ribs are healing. You'll know when they've re-bounded."

"How long?" Hannah asked, realizing her workload

at home wouldn't stop just because she was injured.

"Several weeks," he said. "But, we'll make that determination at your next appointment."

"It feels better already," Hannah said after the band was adjusted, and in place.

"When did your husband assault you?"

"The last time was Friday night."

Then, without missing a beat, he continued; as if ignoring her answer. "Let's have a look at those eyes," he said, and scooted his stool closer. "I see several abrasions and rips in the corner of your left eye. There's also some swelling and bruising. The right one isn't so bad." But then he touched her lid with the tip of a gloved finger.

"That hurts." she said, reaching up.

"Just takes time to heal," he said. "But, your lips are already showing signs of healing. The bruising has faded some, which is good. The swelling should go down even more in a couple of days."

Hannah tried to smile, but was more concerned with the throbbing in her broken ribs.

"Here's some salve for the bruising and abrasions," he said. "Apply twice daily." Then he smiled, and patted her lightly on the hand. "Just make sure you wear that elastic brace until released from my care."

"I will," she said, and forced a smile. "Thanks."

"I'll need to see you again, in my office, in two weeks," he said. "Now wait here. I'll be right back."

The alcove where Hannah sat was cold and unfeeling. In silence she stared at the wall, realizing the load she now carried was more than overwhelming.

Jeremy will be so mad that I went to the doctor. But I need documentation. I need proof of this assault.

Her only goal, from this time forward, was getting away from her husband.

***

Later the curtain in the alcove again swung wide, and a deputy sheriff, dressed from top to bottom in uniformed attire, stepped inside. A leather holder by his side revealed the tip of a gun, and his jacket sported several buttons of achievement. Although his demeanor was intimidating, Hannah could only pray he was there to help her.

"I understand you were assaulted Friday night," he said.

"Yes—by my husband."

"Can you tell me about it?"

Then, as unrestrained tears silently slid down her face, Hannah re-told the happenings of Friday past.

"How many times have you been assaulted?"

"A lot," she said, as tears continued to flow.

"How long have you been married?"

"Almost twelve years," she said, again twisting her hands. Her fingers, now red, were also raw from gripping them.

"You know it's against the law for a husband to beat his wife."

"I didn't know," she said, again lowering her eyes.

"Well, it is," he said, then took a step forward; still fingering his gun holster. "My advice to you is get away from your husband. Move out. Find someone who will help you get away from this man. Whatever it takes."

"I'm planning to leave when the kids get out of school this summer," she said, glancing up.

"You need to get away now. Right now."

A jolt of fear then raced through her body.

"You can go to a woman's shelter," he said. "I'll give you an address if you'll take it."

"I don't know—"

Jeremy will feel betrayed. But maybe, for once, I need to think about myself, and the kids.

"Is there someone in the family who can take you in?"

"Maybe—maybe my mother-in-law. Actually, I'm staying at her house right now."

"That may not be a good idea," he said. "Is there anyone else?"

"No, not really. My parents don't live close."

"That's okay," he said, biting his lip. "But once you get a restraining order, you can move back to your own place, and then your husband can't touch you."

"Are you sure?" she asked, but then squirmed under his gaze as he again fingered his holster.

"Yes," he said "I'm sure."

His words were now holding her attention. But her lips were again dry, so she ran her tongue over them to moisten them. Then she shifted in her seat, still trying to find a more comfortable position as explosions of fractured pain rippled through her rib cage.

"You'll need an attorney to file a restraining order," he said, shifting again.

"How?"

"I'll give you an attorney's card. Call him today and make an appointment. In the meantime, stay away from our house, and your husband. My advice is not to say anything to anyone until you get some papers for protection."

"I—I'll try."

"If you want to stay alive, you will."

In that instant Hannah decided to make it work—at least until the restraining order was signed. Already she knew how keep a secret. When papers were served, everyone would be surprised.

She drew a deep breath, grabbed her side, and then looked deeply into the man's eyes. "Thanks," she said, a hint of a smile forming on split lips. "I think you are an answer to prayer."

Black eyes, broken bones, and swollen lips can be treated. But fractured emotions need healing too. After all, make-up can't hide everything.

Chapter Twenty-Five

Rubber Meets the Road

Parked in front of Hannah's house were two cars. Adrenalin high, she cut the ignition to her, removed the key, and stumbled out. Her hands were now crimson red, but more from her grip than the cold. Climbing the porch steps was Jeremy. Following behind was a deputy sheriff.

In an instant she realized this scene wasn't designed to unfold in her presence. The timing of her arrival home had been misjudged. Still she remained glued to the asphalt, unable to move.

Her legs, now weak, began to buckle, as fear, anxiety, and panic surrounded her; leaving her anchored to the moment. Tears of both frustration and anger were then blinked away, and she leaned against the car for support.

What should I do? I should leave. But, I can't move.

Twelve years. Abused for twelve years. Although alone and frightened, her resolution was solid. Her mind was made up. The decision to force separation on her husband was a must, or she would face certain death.

The sheriff's department had been more sympathetic than local police, who never once believed her reports. But, why would they? The chief of police, as later learned, was related to Jeremy.

Her heart ached for her mother-in-law. By now Mrs. Allen must realize her son was a wife beater.

Also, at this point Hannah's self-esteem was so low she wanted to die. But death was not the legacy she desired to leave her children. For them alone she would stand strong, Hannah's and refuse to again accept weak promises and undeserved threats.

It was over—finally. For once the legal system had worked. After hiring an attorney, a restraining order was obtained, and Jeremy ordered from the house. Only then could Hannah safely return with the children.

Rick, somewhat concerned, later pulled the pens on Jeremy's guns; thus rendering them unusable. Still, unspeakable terror remained as Hannah's separation only triggered more terrorization through stalking.

TEMPORARY ORDER
FOR EMERGENCY RELIEF
UNDER CHAPTER 50 OF THE
GENERAL STATUTES OF NORTH CAROLINA

This cause coming on to be heard and being heard before the undersigned District Court Judge Presiding, and being heard upon plaintiff's motion for emergency relief, as provided by Chapter 50 of the General Statutes.

And it having been made to appear to the Court and the Court finding as a fact from the plaintiff's verified Complaint the following:

1.

That the Plaintiff and Defendant are citizens and residents of Randolph County

2.

That the Plaintiff and Defendant are husband and wife

3.

That the Plaintiff reasonably figures she is in danger of imminent serious bodily injury as a consequence of the Defendant's history of violent acts towards her.

4.

That the Defendant has assaulted the Plaintiff and caused serious bodily injury in that the defendant has beaten the Plaintiff on several occasions during the course of the marriage; the latest being on December 31; that the Defendant has a violent temper, and has threatened the kill the Plaintiff on a number of occasions.

5.

That the Plaintiff has an immediate need of shelter and security and support, to be provided for by the marital residence, and the furnishings therein, and also the Honda automobile, free from the interference and harassment of the Defendant.

6.

That the demonstrated behavior of the Defendant is such as to constitute good cause of the belief that the plaintiff is in immediate and present danger of domestic violence at the hands of the defendant

CONCLUSIONS OF LAW

That the Court has jurisdiction of the subject matter and of the parties to this cause

2.

That the Plaintiff is entitled to an immediate temporary order for emergency relief to protect her and minor children from the interference, harassment, and violence of the defendant, and to provide a secure residence for her free from the interference and harassment of the Defendant pending further hearing of this cause; that this cause should be calendared for hearing within 10 days from the filing of the Complaint and Motion for Emergency Relief, and the execution of this order.

IT IS THEREFORE ORDERED,
ADJUDGED, AND DECREED:

1.

The Defendant be and is hereby ordered to henceforth refrain from all acts of violence and threats of violence towards the Plaintiff and the minor children, and all direct and indirect acts of interference with or harassment of the Plaintiff and minor children;

2.

That the Plaintiff be and is hereby awarded immediate and exclusive temporary possession of the marital residence, and the furnishings located therein, and of the Honda automobile titled in both names all free of interference from and harassment by the Defendant;

3.

That the Defendant be and is hereby ordered to appear before the Honorable Judge Presiding of the District Court at 9:30 o'clock a.m. on Friday, January 17, or as soon thereafter as the Defendant might be heard, for a hearing on the Plaintiff's motion for emergency relief.

4.

That a copy of this order is served upon the Defendant, and a copy of the order to be delivered to the appropriate law enforcement agencies as provided by Chapter 50B of the North Carolina General Statutes.

IN THE GENERAL COURT OF JUSTICE
DISTRICT COURT DIVISION
COMPLAINT

The Plaintiff, complaining of the Defendant, alleges and says:

1.

That the Plaintiff and the Defendant are citizens and residents of North Carolina

2.

That the Plaintiff and Defendant were married to each other on June 20

3.

That there are three children of the marriage, to wit: Haley, born October 18, Austin, born February 20, and Matthew, born May 10

4.

That the Plaintiff is a faithful and dutiful wife, and has done nothing to provoke the behavior of the Defendant as herein alleged.

5.

That the Plaintiff is a dependent spouse within the meaning of Chapter 50 of the General Statues of North Carolina

6.

That the Defendant is a supporting spouse within the meaning of Chapter 50 of the General Statutes of North Carolina.

7.

That the Plaintiff is a fit and proper person to have the care, custody, and control of the minor children, and it is in the best interest of the minor children that she has care, custody, and control of said minor children.

8.

That the Defendant has committed such indignities to the person of the Plaintiff as to render her life burdensome and her condition intolerable by engaging in the following course and pattern of conduct:

(a) That the Defendant has assaulted and beaten the Plaintiff on an number of occasions, the latest being December 31, said beatings being of such severity that the Plaintiff has had to seek medical treatment, and is still under the care of a physician as a result of the beatings inflicted upon her by the Defendant;

(b) That the Defendant has verbally abused the Plaintiff, both within and outside the presence of the minor children, and has used vulgar and indecent language directed towards the Plaintiff on numbers of occasions;

(c) That the Defendant has threatened to kill the Plaintiff, and has threatened to kidnap the children of the parties;

(d) That the Defendant has advised the Plaintiff that he has slept with several other women, and that he did not love the Plaintiff anymore;

(e) That the Defendant has, on several occasions, thrown projectiles towards the Plaintiff, including pieces of wood, and has damaged articles of property in the house, in fits of rage;

(f) That the Defendant has kept the Plaintiff and the children awake into the wee hours of the morning on numbers of occasions, with his cursing's and carrying on;

(g) That the Defendant has generally put the Plaintiff in fear for her life and the lives of her children by his actions.

9.

The Defendant constructively abandoned the Plaintiff, forcing her out of the marital home, in fear for her life, and for the safety of her children.

10.

That the Plaintiff and the Defendant are co-owners of a marital residence, and the Plaintiff is in need of an order permitting her to reside therein, along with possession of all the furniture located therein.

11.

That the Plaintiff and Defendant are joint owners of a Honda automobile, which has been driven primarily by the Plaintiff; that the Plaintiff is in need of an immediate order allowing her continued possession of said Honda

12.

That the Defendant is capable of providing support for the Plaintiff and the minor children, both on a temporary and permanent basis, and the Plaintiff is in need of substantial support for herself, and the minor children

13.

That the acts of the Defendant, in intentionally causing bodily injury to the Plaintiff, and placing the Plaintiff in fear of imminent serious bodily injury by the threat of killing her, or such acts, under G.S. 50B et. seq., that entitles the Plaintiff to temporary emergency relief.

WHEREFORE, the Plaintiff prays:

1.

That she be granted a divorce from bed and board from the Defendant.

2.

That she be granted an order of reasonable alimony, both on a temporary and permanent basis.

3.

That she be granted the general care, custody, and control of the minor children of the marriage, with the Defendant being required to pay an adequate amount of support for said children, both on a temporary and permanent basis;

4.

That she be granted the sole and exclusive use and possession of the former marital residence of the parties, along with the furnishings located therein, along with the Honda automobile which is titled in both names;

5.

That a temporary order for emergency relief be issued pursuant to Chapter 50B of the General Statutes of North Carolina.

6.

That this verified complaint be treated as an affidavit within this cause and in support of her motion for temporary and emergency relief.

7.

For such other relief as the Court deems just and proper.

***

Jeremy neither denied nor appealed his court ordered documents as his true character had been revealed. The money he shared from his cashed-in retirement paid for an attorney, and bought Hannah's freedom. The money he kept for himself purchased a brand new car.

Chapter Twenty-Six

Discarded Memories

An unexpected knock at the door caused an insatiable panic to surface. Hannah, standing behind the door, grabbed her heart, and began to tremble. Was it Jeremy? If so, she couldn't let him in.

Now terrified, she cautiously pulled a corner of the closed curtain aside, and peeked through the window. Her mother and Aunt Rose had never looked so good.

"Am I ever glad to see you two," she said, instantly springing into action. Her joy then resonated beyond a smile as she reached through the door, grabbed them both, and pulled them inside.

Aunt Rose, after learning of her dilemma, had urged her mother to drive the distance, and offer assistance if needed. But in Hannah's mind, they were simply angels sent to guard her. Now she wouldn't need to face her demons alone. Jeremy, at last, wouldn't disregard his restraining order, and she could leave the children in their care while at work. And, for the first time in a long time, she felt safe under her own roof. Reinforcements had arrived.

***

Once home Hannah peeled her coat off, laid it across her arm, then walked across the kitchen tiles. But the sound of her own footsteps echoed back as she continued her stride. "I'm home from work," she said, then watched as Matthew scampered across the floor to greet her.

Then, from the next room, a voice spoke. "Guess who came by today."

"Don't know," she said, then gave the baby a hug. But when she glanced up, her mother was in the kitchen.

"It was one of your sisters-in-law," she said.

"What did she want?" Hannah asked, as feelings of apprehension crept up her spine.

"She said her brother needed some clothes. He didn't get them all when the police picked him up."

Unrestrained fear then whipped into action, and Hannah began to shake uncontrollably. She then scanned the room, hoping nothing more than clothes. Her bond with Jeremy's family was fast fading, and she knew it. Not one word from any one of them since their court-ordered separation.

"What else did she take?" she asked, as her eyes again roamed the room.

"I don't know what she took," her mother said. "Some clothes, I guess."

"Why didn't you stay with her?" Hannah asked. And, out of nervousness, picked up a sock, and tossed it in the laundry basket. Then she jerked the closet door open. It was bare. Only a few dresses remained, but had been shoved in a corner. The next instant she turned, and opened the bureau drawers.

"Mother, why didn't you watch her?" Hannah's words then conveyed her despair, and she squeezed back hot tears. "She took my picture discs. They're all gone."

"I didn't see what she took," her mother said, then sat down on the edge of the bed. "I guess I trusted her."

"You can't always trust people," Hannah said, as frustration again took center stage. An escaped tear was then wiped away. "Especially now."

"Maybe you can get them back."

"I doubt it," Hannah said. "I'll probably never get them back."

But her mother's calmness was irritating, so she cleared her throat, and took a deep breath. The next instant she was pacing the floor—creating an uneven path between wooden blocks and colorful Lego's. It was difficult to believe her sister-in-law had taken her pictures—stolen them was more like it. *I can't believe this is happening. What next?*

"I think I'll call Ashley," she said, thinking out loud. She picked up the phone, and then punched in the number. But minutes later the piece dropped.

"What did she say," Aunt Rose asked.

"She gave them to Jeremy," Hannah said, as angry tears were brushed away. "He has them now."

"Why would she take those, of all things?" her mother asked.

"I have no idea," Hannah said. But her words were automatic, and she continued to pace the floor.

"The only thing men are good for is giving us babies," Aunt Rose quipped.

Still angry tears flowed, and gathered on Hannah's blouse as intense hurt and deep frustration were unleashed.

"I'll never see those pictures again," she said. "I just know it." And again she wiped more tears away. "Those were my memories—pictures of my children so creatively captured."

She sat down, and held her head in her hand. "Will this pain ever end?" she whispered. "And how could Ashley do this to me—a sister-in-law who is more like a sister?"

Yet deep in her heart, Hannah knew those pictures were forever gone—just like her marriage.

And, they were.

Chapter Twenty-Seven

On Notice

Monday came, and Hannah mentally readied herself to turn in a two-week notice. She was also preparing to move back home with her parents. Although reluctant, they had agreed to her request.

Although only three months employed at Health Aid Medical, yet she dreaded giving it up. But could she survive those two weeks while working a notice? She still feared Jeremy's harassment in public—even worse, his threat to kill her.

Nights were more than nightmares. Jeremy's disregard for his restraining order brought new bouts of fear to Hannah's already disrupted life. Already he had materialized at gas stations, supermarkets, and convenience stores when she was there. But since it was doubtful local police would uphold the order, she decided not to contact them. Disbelief had jilted her before.

She was also terrorized Jeremy would kidnap the children from school—another reason for panic. A copy of her separation agreement was now in the hands of school personnel, and provided some comfort. But not enough. Although warned, could they be trusted to keep her children away from him?

A lack of faith in others had again surfaced, as loss of sleep and fear of the unknown claimed her sanity. Now stressed to the max, she sagged beneath the emotional load she now carried. Her body, still healing from Jeremy's last assault, also resisted food despite a desire to keep her strength up. Although the first step in her plan was behind her, she remained frightened, tense, and nervous. Running on fumes of fear, anxiety, and dread allowed what energy she had to quickly fade once home from work each day.

"Jeremy's removal from the house didn't stop everything," she said under her breath while climbing the stairs to her office.

"He's downstairs," a gruff voice said, from below. "What do you want me to do?"

"Please. Don't let him come up," she said, shaking.

"Done."

She leaned against the office door for support, but felt instant paralysis. The sound of running footsteps then caught her attention, and she watched as the salesman burst into view.

"He's gone," he said, quite out of breath.

Then, somehow, her legs regained enough strength to carry her to a chair in the office. But then her knees buckled, and her body began to shake. "What happened?" she asked, then rubbed the brace on her ribs.

"We ran him off," he said. "Told him to never come here again, and to leave you alone." And then he grinned.

"Thanks a million," was all Hannah could manage as nerves again rattled beneath her skin. But her legs, still weak, remained pulp beneath her.

***

A couple of hours later the receptionist placed a vase full of aromatic flowers on Hannah's desk. "Look what the florist just delivered," she said, and a smile covered her face. "Aren't these roses gorgeous?"

"For me?" Again Hannah's heart pounded in disbelief. *Did Jeremy just send me flowers?*

"Wow! A dozen red roses," the receptionist said. "You must be special to someone."

"Who sent them?"

"Look at the card."

Hannah's hands again trembled as she pulled the insert from a tiny envelope.

"They're from my husband," she said. Then, on wobbly legs, she walked through the door to the trash can, ready to dump the arrangement.

"What are you doing?" the receptionist asked, and quickly grabbed her heart. "Don't throw them away."

Hannah turned, and pushed the vase back into her hands. "Then you take them," she said.

"Don't you want them?"

"No. No, I don't."

The receptionist's eyebrows lifted. "Are you sure?" she asked.

"Yes. I'm sure."

"Then I'll put them in the front office for everyone to enjoy," she said.

"As long as I don't have to look at them."

"You must really be mad at your husband."

But Hannah only turned away. "He won't be my husband for long," she whispered. Rubber legs carried her back to her office.

"Whew," she said, grabbing her sore ribs and slowly releasing new air. "Thank God for adrenalin, and a rib brace."

Chapter Twenty-Eight

Moving On

Snow in the forecast did not deter Hannah's plans. As intended, and still on target, Friday would be her last day at Health Aid Medical. Somehow she was managing a two-week notice.

Rick had insisted she rent a large truck. He and Emily would be her driving team. They felt it best if she and Jeremy separated, and decided to assist in the move.

***

Hannah handed the key to Rick for truck pick-up. But with that action she also surrendered to emotions of jubilation. Already packed boxes were then shoved into the trailer along with household items, boxes of clothing, and toys. Furniture placed against other pieces in the van soon filled the remaining gaps.

Everything would be needed for the children, so Hannah was cleaning house. Well, almost. Jeremy's request for the large screen television, and their bedroom set, would be honored.

A recliner, ministry materials, books, and several snapshots of the kids would also remain for his return to their home. A large writing desk, given as a gift, would also remain. Reminders of the life she once had were best left behind.

Saturday morning, after the final box was loaded, Hannah's caravan began winding its way through town.

From behind the wheel of the U-Haul, Rick grinned and then waved. Her car, packed, to the max, followed close behind. Emily, at the rear, ended the motorcade.

Although smiling to show elation, on the inside Hannah remained demur. And when her car rolled from the curb, tender tears were blinked away. Three children were staying behind with Grams, and a non-caring husband—if only for the week-end. Words of praise and uplifting prayer would remain on her lips as her venture began to unfold.

Her new life, now well under way, was falling into place as if divinely orchestrated. Success was beckoning her forward, allowing happiness to again surface despite a serious lack of resources at destination's end.

Because she had survived the worst of times, things could only get better. Now was not a time of worry. Now was a time of rejoicing.

Sunday afternoon Jeremy returned the children to Hannah at her parent's home, as previously planned. And so began a new era in her life.

***

Due to an overly restrictive background Hannah was anchored to a marriage that should have ended long before it began. The dictators in her life were long overbearing, demanding, and restraining. But after realizing the judgments of others had been unrealistic, she was more than ready to move forward.

With limited human intervention, she had escaped a cruel and violent marriage. Her husband, now tamed with legal restraints, had been removed from her life. And the children were content, and happy. What more could she ask?

Later, after the dust had settled, Hannah realized God was still on her side. Her escape had been swift, and uneventful. And, for the first time in years, she was relieved, content, and happier than ever before. Because "...the steps of a good man (or woman) are ordered by the LORD, and He delights in his way" (Psalms 37:23)

Chapter Twenty-Nine

Miracles

The home of Hannah's parent's, now a haven of retreat, was also a place of new beginnings.

"Come on, kids," Hannah said. "It's time to go." Still stressed, her brow wrinkled as she hustled Haley and Austin out the door.

But before she left, she kissed Matthew, and then squeezed him tight. "Be good for Grandmother," she said. "I'm only taking your brother and sister to sign up for school. But, we'll be back soon. You can go yourself in a couple of years." Then she walked out the door, ready to greet the world at the primary school.

But Matthew stared longingly out the window as her car backed down the frozen hill.

Crusty snow covered the ground, and glistened in the brisk sunlight as Hannah car headed out. Several scraped piles, laden with dirt and debris, remained on the side of already scraped roads, and hinted at the temperature outside. The car, icy to the touch, bounced over frozen bumps and sunken potholes as her small family trucked along.

Registering Haley and Austin in school was yet another step in the plan. Enrolling them would seal their destiny, and hold her to the plan. The next hurdle would be finding a job. At last she was ready to ditch her scars, and move forward in a new direction.

***

The office at Amelia Primary looked daunting. Still Hannah pressed forward, trusting an inner instinct to retain a positive attitude. She was also desperate for friends. Reaching out to everyone along the way would be a start. Her new endeavor was then embraced with a prayer on her lips, and hope in her heart.

"Do you want to enroll your children in school?" the receptionist asked after she stepped inside the main office.

"This is Haley, and Austin," Hannah said, pointing. "And yes, we do." She reached in her pocket, pulled out a tattered envelope, and then placed it in the lady's hand. Still, in her haste to retreat, she had somehow remembered to request the children's school records before their move.

"Are you employed?" the lady asked.

"No—no not yet," Hannah said. "I'm recently separated." Instantly the chair beneath her felt stiff, and she took a deep breath; realizing new patterns of descriptive responses were being created.

"I get child support," she said, lips trembling.

"How much?"

"Four-hundred a month."

"Then your kids qualify for the free lunch program."

A lopsided smile again swathed Hannah's face. "That's great," she said. "I didn't know you had a free lunch program." At least her children would have good food to eat. Worry over their hunger was now eased.

"Thank you, Lord," she whispered softly.

Again another deep breath and she pressed forward. "I'm looking for a job," she said, and her voice quavered. On the inside she wanted to vomit as fear had again surfaced.

"As a matter of fact," the lady said, "an Office Manager is needed at Hadley Optional School."

"Hadley Optional School? I thought it closed years ago."

"It did. But the county re-opened, this time as a non-traditional optional primary—for kindergarten through fifth."

"How do I apply?" Words of confidence came from

nowhere. Where they hers?

"Go to the Board of Education and fill out an application," the lady said. "You'll also need two references." Then she fingered her rolodex. "Here's the number and address," she said, pointing. "I'll write them down for you."

"Thanks. You've been more than helpful," Hannah said, and again smiled.

"The principal will need to interview you too."

"Oh—okay. Thanks."

"I hope everything works out," the lady said.

"So do I."

"It's been two weeks since that job was first listed," she said. "And, surprise—surprise, it hasn't yet filled."

Again her smile was warming, and Hannah's heart filled with new hope.

"It's unusual a job opening in the school system doesn't immediately fill."

"Thanks again," Hannah said. But on the inside she was jubilant, causing her words to gush.

"And since there's snow on the ground, make sure to watch the news for school attendance."

"Just like when I attended this same school years ago."

"Exactly the same."

"Thanks," Hannah said, and her smile was instant. "Thanks for the information."

The lady turned, and then grinned at Haley and Austin. "I guess you're excited about going to a new school," she said. And immediately their heads bobbed up and down, a sure sign that change was good.

"This is a great school—one of the best. Jerry Greenspan is a wonderful principal. You'll enjoy coming every day."

Hannah turned, and then reached for the children's coats. The pressure in her head then seemed to ease. "Put these on," she said, smiling. "It's cold outside."

"Good luck on your job hunt," the lady said.

"Thanks again, Hannah said. "I've been filling out applications all week, but no luck."

"Maybe this is the job for you."

In her heart Hannah prayed it was. But who could she use for job references? Twelve years since living in her home town, and her list of former friends had dwindled to none. But then she recalled a former church member she had used as a reference years before. He wouldn't mind if she did again. But who else could she use? She prayed God would provide.

***

The words County Board of Education were inscribed on the dark brick of an old school building now used as administrative offices for the school Superintendent, and other related positions. It was the hub of all educational operations in the county.

In silence Hannah stared at the old building, prayers again rolling from her lips that all would go well with her quest. She took a deep breath, turned, and, with bold determination, climbed wide cement steps that lead to multiple entry doors.

As she stepped inside, the heaviness of aged wood released a musty smell after she swung them open. Inside, the hallways echoed their emptiness around her, a reminder of school days as a child. But when she heard footsteps clacking on the old planked floor, she quickly refocused. A man was striding toward her. It was a former teacher, Mr. Howard, who had taught co-operative office practice when she was in high school. From him she had learned office machine operations, as well as secretarial skills.

"Hello, Mr. Howard."

"Hannah, how are you?"

"You remember me," she said, and grinned—both inside and out. *Things might be looking up after all.*

"Of course I do,' he said. "I never forget my students."

Then, from down the hallway, the muffled drone of keyboards, muted voices, and spurts of laughter echoed through closed doors. Hannah, still overcome with her new life, wanted to pinch herself.

"What brings you here?" he asked.

"To fill out an application for the job at Hadley Optional School," she said, all the while praying he wouldn't notice her nervousness. "Could I use you for a reference?"

"Of course you can," he said, then pointed to the second door on the right. "Just go in that room, and someone will give you an application." And, with a smile, he reached out his hand for a quick shake. "Good luck," he said; then turned on his heel, and walked away.

But now she had two references, and did a little two-step. Mr. Howard was a good one. Maybe she had a shot at this job after all.

A couple of hours later, when she stepped inside Gray Optional School, she couldn't help but smile. The voices echoing around her were pleasant, and embracing, and she glowed from their exuberance. Chatter from classrooms down the hallway also made the environment an exciting place to be.

A pretty lady with short, dark hair and hints of gray greeted her. "Hello. I'm Mrs. Foster, the school principal," she said. "Can I help you?"

"I'm looking for a job," Hannah said. "I was told you needed an Office Manager."

"Come into my office, and have a seat," she said, "and tell me a little bit about yourself." Then, minutes later, she asked the question Hannah longed to hear. "When can you come to work?"

"When do you need me?"

"How about tomorrow morning at 7:30?"

"I'll be here," Hannah said. And, although shaking on the outside, she was leaping on the inside.

"I knew the minute you walked in the door you were the one for the job," Mrs. Foster said. "I've been waiting for the right person to fill this position for two weeks." Again she reached out her hand. And, with a firm shake, the deal was sealed.

"I'll see you first thing in the morning," she said.

Hannah was elated. "The sun is shining all over the world," she sang in soft undertones after stepping back outside. *Two weeks. The exact amount of time I was working her two-week notice before moving. God was holding this job for me.*

"Pack your bags and leave." Jeremy's spoken words had long ago shattered her trusting heart. But after hearing them again and again, she had finally taken the initiative. After all, wasn't obey one of her marriage vows?

Her only regret was not leaving the union earlier. But everyone trusts a preacher. If he couldn't be trusted, then who could? And who would think the pastor of a church could also be an abuser? It just wasn't believed.

Scripture in the Bible became Hannah's consolation. And, as revelations of God's truth were revealed, she realized that her once silenced cries had truly heard.

"For such people are false apostles, deceitful workers, masquerading as apostles of Christ. And no wonder, for Satan himself masquerades as an angel of light. It is not surprising, then, if his servants also masquerade as servants of righteousness" (2 Corinthians 11:13-15)

At last she was free—free from a man who often lashed out with a vengeance, and terrorized her life.

"...He said to me, "My grace is sufficient for you, for my power is made perfect in weakness" (2 Corinthians 12:9)

But as more words from the Bible lifted Hannah's spirit, her joy manifested in song and praise.

Chapter Thirty

A Place of Her Own

The home where Hannah's parent's lived was way too small for all of them under the same roof. Hannah's intent, however, was to never sponge off them, but move out as soon as possible. She also realized that finding her own place would again cut the umbilical cord, and provide the confidence needed to stand on her own two feet.

"Who is it?" she mouthed when her mother answered the phone. Three rings were enough to send her into a tailspin. Was it Jeremy? She prayed it wasn't. His calls were callous, and he continued pounding her with threats. Promises to kidnap the children were a constant obstacle of dread.

But after a huge gulp, she tried to calm herself. Her stomach, still tied in knots, began to rumble and churn. She dreaded the jarring ring of the phone—fearing yet another threat. Would she ever feel normal again? Living on the edge was still an everyday occurrence.

"It's Abby, your old childhood friend," her mother said, then handed Hannah the phone.

"Hi, Abby," Hannah said, but then her voice cracked. "I'm glad it's you and not my Ex."

"How's the job hunt going?" Abby asked.

"Oh, I found one," Hannah said, and her excitement spilled over as this bit of news was relayed. "At Hadley Optional School—today." Still, she couldn't help but smile out loud. The joy in her heart was simply therapeutic.

"I love that little school," Abby said. "What's your job

title?"

"Bookkeeper, secretary, office lady, receptionist, Band-Aid applier" Hannah said, and a small giggle rapped around her tongue. "I guess I'll have many titles—Office Manager being the first. It's a small school, you know."

"You'll enjoy working there," Abby said. "I have friends whose children attended a couple of years ago."

"By the way," Hannah said, "I've been looking in the paper for an apartment to rent." Then, as her heart palpations slowed, she began to relax. Each new beat was now more rhythmic than the last.

"Have you called Brighton Hill Apartments?" Abby was prodding her along.

"Never heard of it," Hannah said, then plopped down on the sofa for a long chat.

"You can probably afford this one," Abby said. "It's near Hendersonville."

Still nervous, Hannah shifted positions. "How much is the rent?"

"Its government subsidized. The rent depends on your salary."

"That sounds good—really good," Hannah said. "Is it listed in the phone book?" And instantly a calming peace settled in her heart, and she quietly lifted the book; then absentmindedly leafed through the pages.

"My friend Libby used to live there," Abby said.

"Did she like it?"

"She said it was really nice, with a playground." Abby then paused. "There's usually a long waiting list. It took Libby a long time to get an apartment."

Hannah's jaw dropped. "A waiting list?" Still, it was worth checking out. Maybe, just maybe...

***

When the apartment manager handed Hannah a set of keys to a four-bedroom apartment on the first floor, she almost exploded with excitement.

"There's usually a long waiting list before an apartment comes available," the manager said. "But, you got lucky. The keys to this one were turned in this morning. It takes two days to have it cleaned. You can move in this week-end."

Hannah tried not to dance a jig.

"You also qualify for a discount in your monthly rent," the manager said after opening the door. "Just make sure their part is paid on time."

It was difficult for Hannah to restrain her excitement. Only thirty days living with her parents, and she now had her own place. She could hardly wait to share the news with her children. At that moment she was both joyful and ecstatic, and the happier than she had been in years.

Refrains of melody filled her heart with rapture as the shattered pieces of her existence fell into place. Whitney Houston's song *The Greatest Love of All* spoke to her heart, as love for her own self began to surface. As horrific as life had been, nothing compared to knowing that God was still on her side. His provision surrounded her, and the children, as together they embarked on their new lives with enthusiasm, and unwavering peace.

***

Brighton Hill Apartments provided the perfect place for a battered woman to begin again. After the dust had settled, Hannah's family of four soared into peaceful routines of daily living. A permanent reprieve from violence was simply heaven on earth. Even more noticeable were the calming effects of waking up and going to sleep in peace. They could come and go at will without fear of sabotage.

The happiest days of Hannah's life were now before her. Her imprisoned existence was over, and she was, as last, free from the bondage of hostility.

Then, as the Holy Spirit wrapped His arms around her, confidence in her own self opened the door to pure bliss. Soon a church was found where songs of consolation could minister to her weary, and fractured heart.

Downpours of new rain were eagerly embraced as huge droplets splattered the ground around her. She soaked in the sunshine as it streamed countless rays of glamour upon her. And she reveled in newfound friendships as her new beginnings were embraced.

Life's darkest storm had passed, the sky was again blue, and the world a brighter place to be.

Chapter Thirty-One

Too Close for Comfort

Jeremy's visits with the children following Hannah's recent court documents had been pre-arranged. He would pick them up Friday afternoon at her childhood home, thus reducing any risk of altercation. Her parents, somewhat hesitant, again promised to oversee the operation.

Earlier in the afternoon, after her move to the apartment, Hannah's little ones were dropped off at her parent's home; and she drove away. Her plan—not to be anywhere Jeremy was.

But as she meandered back down the road toward the apartment, she lazily glanced in the rear-view mirror. Horror then collided with terror. His car was advancing, and memories of former threats instantly held her hostage. Her heart again leaped to her throat. She was now in full panic mode. But why was he following her?

Seconds later his car slid up beside hers, and he motioned her over. And instantly her strength dissolved. *What can I do? And do I even have a choice? God, please help me.*

Her body began to tremble—so violently the car began to wobble. She realized the risk was great. The freedom she had worked so hard to achieve—liberty from her assailant—was again crumbling at her feet.

With strong reservation she steered the car into a gas station, applied the break, but allowed the engine to run. Again her body sagged as shock from the drama now unfolding before her was intense. Then, with heart in throat she uttered a quick prayer for safety, and prepared to see Jeremy—face to face.

The next instant he jumped from his car, and strode to hers. But as he stepped closer, she reached over and locked the door. And, as a precaution, rolled the window half-way down. She was more than cautious—still fearing for her life. Not only was her body dripping with sweat, but her hands continued to tremble.

"Why are you following me?" she asked, then gripped the steering wheel tight. Then reaching deep inside, she prayed for calmness and more strength. "I thought you were getting the kids."

Jeremy moved closer to the window. "I'll still get them," he said, "but I wanted to see you first."

"You don't need to see me," she said. Still horrified, her knees began to knock together in bone-chilling rhythm. She prayed he wouldn't notice.

"I want you back, Han."

"No." Although petrified, her voice came across as harsh, and decisive. Then she shifted in the seat, still uncomfortable and vulnerable.

"You never talk to me on the phone," he said. "I want you back."

Still she remained silent.

"If you come back, I'll give you everything you what."

"No." Bracing gulps of air were then inhaled as she tied to stay composed.

"How about some new clothes."

"No." Still holding her ground, Hannah slid away from the window.

"You can have my new car. Anything you want."

"It's over." And her lips pulled into a thin line. "Our marriage is over."

"I want you back."

But the tone in his voice, and the look on his face, brought new bouts of dread to her already dwindling courage, and she shivered in fear.

"The children need me."

Panic delayed a response, but she gripped the wheel even tighter.

"We'll take a trip together," Jeremy said. "I've got tickets to the Bahamas from being best salesman this month." His lips then curved. "I won't ever hit you again—I promise. We can start over."

How many times has he said that?

"No." Her words were bold. But on the inside she was proud.

"Then I'll—I'll move here with you."

Conflicting dread instantly rose up in Hannah's throat. His words had again stirred insurmountable fear. Would she ever get beyond this terror?

"Please, don't." Her words were tempered.

But he put his hand out as if to stop her. "Just think about it," he said. Then stepping closer, he rotated his hand in a circular motion. "Roll the window all the way down."

Still she cowered in her seat. "No. Just leave me alone."

"I want to kiss you."

"I don't think so." Again her body quivered, and she searched for the window control.

"Don't close the window yet."

"We have nothing more to discuss. Please, just go away." Bu even to herself, her words were strangely cold.

"You know I still love you," he said. Still his tallness was intimidating as his flashed his famous smile.

"Yeah, right," she wanted to say. "Still lying?" Instead she bit her tongue. Still unwavering in her commitment to never return to her old life, she refused submission. She didn't want him. And, it really was over. She couldn't help but smile. On the inside she was jubilant.

"Why are you smiling?" He looked confused.

"Huh? Oh—nothing."

"Where do you live? I want to come by and see you, and the kids"

Fear instantly jerked Hannah into action. "No." Although petrified, the sternness in her own voice kept her grounded. "You have the kids every other week-end. You don't get me."

"Why won't you give me another chance?" Jeremy's words were agitated.

How she hated his begging—his pleading.

"No. It's over. Just go away and leave me alone."

The next instant she slapped the control, and the window shot up. But on the inside, she was more than proud. *Thank God he didn't assault me in the parking lot.*

But she know too many stories that ended with a dead wife, so she remained fearful of his next move. But maybe, just maybe, their separation would hold up after all. She prayed it would.

Sweat again rolled down her back as her car jetted back across the highway. Still terrified, she peeked in the rear view mirror. His car was going in the opposite direction, and she breathed a long sigh of relief.

"Thank you, Lord," she said out loud. Yet she needed miles of distance between them. Her heart was again beating at a fast pace, and she took deep breaths, trying to calm back down. Yet somehow she resisted the urge to push the gas petal to the floor; but only because she wanted to stay alive for the children.

The light ahead rotated to orange, and she slowed the car to a stop. Then, while she waited, she rolled the window half-way down, and breathed in the fresh mountain air. In the distance, the tranquility of snow covered peaks, and the chill of winter, helped to clear her head.

As a mother, Hannah always expected the worst when Jeremy drove away with the children. "Please protect them and bring them back safe and sound," she prayed, realizing they would see their dad in the next few minutes.

"I'll just leave everything in God's hands," she whispered. "Mine are way too limp."

Thirty-Two

Protected

A few weeks into the new job and Hannah was more than jubilant. Internal happiness now filled her life with joy. Things were going well, work was easy to learn, and she enjoyed the environment of school staff and students—often thinking of the little learners as her own.

Early Monday morning she headed down the hallway to a classroom, the heels on her shoes clacking loudly on the hardened tile. Her thoughts then meandered from shoes to kids. She would enroll Haley and Austin in Hadley Optional next year, and pull them out of Amelia Primary.

Glancing around, she noted several pieces of student artwork haphazardly plastered on the wall. Now interested, she stopped, and quietly examined them. In her head she pretended the work belonged to her own children. How they would love this small school with all its pomp and variety. Students sharing common interests, close friendships, and camaraderie would be perfect for her small family. Now smiling, she continued her trek.

The next instant she refocused. The worn-out soles on her two-inch heels were sliding, and she instinctively grabbed the wall to keep from falling. This was something she would need to remember, and take each step with caution. Her shoes were worn out. Cheap five-and-dime types purchased years ago; then used for church, now her only work shoes.

Mrs. Foster earlier mentioned how much her shoes needed re-heeling at a shoe cobbler's. She was a great mentor for sure. Perhaps, Hannah decided, she would do the same. Or, somehow, manage to buy some new ones for her tired, aching feet. But since the worn-out heels were all she owned, she breathed a quick prayer for safety, and continued her errand.

Minutes later, as she sat in the office typing, Mrs. Foster stepped to the door.

"I have a doctor's appointment at eleven," she said, rubbing her shoulder and neck. "Can you handle the office by yourself?"

"Oh, sure," Hannah said. "Don't worry about a thing."

"I'll be back as soon as I can," she said, then shifted her handbag to the other arm. Still looking nervous, she glanced at her watch. "I shouldn't be longer than a couple of hours."

"Are you okay?"

"Just stressed," she said. "New job as school principal, I guess. The last time I saw the doctor, he said stress often generates shoulder and neck pain."

"I hope this time he can help," Hannah said.

Mrs. Foster then turned and fingered her watch band. "I've had quite a bit of pain lately," she said. "I'm going for a re-check, and some stronger medicine."

Hannah's own neck and shoulders ached, and long before the day she launched out on her own. But she couldn't afford a doctor like Mrs. Foster. She would just tough it out. At least, for now, she understood what was causing her own pain—anxiety and stress.

***

The muffled drone of children's voices wafted back from down the hall as Hannah swung the back entry door open. She then stepped outside, and bounded up mature steps. Up ahead, and sitting atop a weathered post for mail collection, was the box. Handling mail was one of her many duties, but she embraced them all with joy in her heart.

She glanced around, then noticed several songbirds

perched atop the handrail crooning the joyful songs of spring. A small planting bed full of yellow jonquils and red tulips adjoining the entrance also looked welcoming to the eye. And, in the distance, several pink and white dogwoods spread their budding blooms for all to see.

But as the fragrance of spring filtered through Hannah's nose, the morning sun reminded her of a loving God; as if a warm blanket of protection covered her. And, for a moment, the weight of fear seemed to lift from her shoulders. Instant joy then flooded her heart. Life was again worth living. God was her protector, provider, and confidant; and, she was content, and happy.

Later, after moments of joyous rapture were embraced, she meandered back down the steps, and into the building. The emotional load she carried was now much lighter than before. Her day was off to a great start.

***

The following day, and just before the school bell rang the dismissal of sixty students, Jeremy's face appeared in an outside window—and Hannah froze. His suit jacket swung in the breeze as he sauntered to the entrance of the small building. And instantly waves of terror overwhelmed her senses, and she stumbled from her desk. Now terrified, she quickly scrambled to Mrs. Foster's office—her designated safety net.

"He's here," Hannah said, still shaking; then grabbed the back of a chair to steady her wobbling legs.

"Your Ex?"

"Yes." Each labored breath was then inhaled and exhaled at an uncalculated speed. "He's walking down the sidewalk," Hannah said, panting. The next instant her energy level dropped and she collapsed on a chair.

"I'll take care of him," Mrs. Foster said. "You wait here." She then strode through the office door, and closed it behind her.

How Hannah hated relying on others for protection.

But, what else could she do? At least someone was willing to step up in her place. "Thank you, God," she whispered. "Thank you, thank you—thank you."

Jeremy was stalking her again. Would she ever feel safe? And what was going on outside the office door? Why was he here? What about the kids?

By the time Mrs. Foster again opened the door, Hannah's breathing was labored. But the principals' smile was encouraging, and Hannah felt instant relief.

"He's gone," Mrs. Foster said. "I don't think he'll be back either."

Still Hannah's stomach rolled as spasms of dread flooded her mind. Then trying to recover, she sat down, and smoothed her skirt. "What happened?" she asked, fear again filtering through her voice.

"I told him that if he ever comes here again, for any reason, I'd have him arrested."

"Thank you," Hannah said, still rubbing her hands. But as her ankles regained strength, her heart felt renewed.

"Now calm down, and get a drink of water," Mrs. Foster said. "I'm sure he won't be back."

***

After work, Hannah glanced around the school—her refuge from the outside world. Again she squeezed herself, making sure she was truly okay. In her mind she felt validated. Someone in authority had stood up to Jeremy, and he caved without a whimper. There wasn't any doubt in her mind why he had come. He would use the excuse of wanting to see the kids. But his true motivation was intimidation.

Still shaken, she left work, ready to pick the children up. Haley and Austin should be at her parents by now, as time for bus drop-off had long passed. It was just a matter of time before she would learn why Jeremy had been at Hadley Optional School.

At the house she watched for even a hint of

expression from her mother as she asked the pointed question, "Do you know who came by the school today?"

"Was it Jeremy?" her mother asked.

Hannah's knees began to buckle, so she grabbed the door for support.

"How did you know?"

"Well, he came by here earlier."

"What?" Hannah was now shaking from head to toe.

"He came to the door and wanted to know where you worked."

"And, you told him?"

"Well, he asked."

"Why?" But now Hannah's legs were rubber. "Why did you tell him?"

"Because, he said he needed to know."

"What else did you tell him?"

Her mother paused, then said, "Well maybe how to get there." But her voice was now guilt ridden—her face ashen.

Still weak, Hannah crumpled in a heap on the sofa. "How could you do that?" she asked. "I thought you understood I was in danger."

"I—I'm sorry."

"He still calls on the phone, and threatens to kill me."

"I'm sorry," her mother said, and then threw her hands in the air before sitting down on a rocking chair. "I can't do anything about that now." She picked up her yarn, looking unconcerned, and began to knit.

"Mother, as I told you before. Never tell him anything."

"I didn't know what to say."

By now Hannah's rage was over the top, but she tried to restrain her rage.

"You didn't have to answer the door."

"He kept knocking," her mother said.

All trust now shattered, Hannah stood on shaky legs. "Come on kids," she said. "Let's go."

Her mother, still knitting, glanced up. "See you tomorrow," she said, waving at Matthew. Haley and Austin had long since retreated.

Although weak and shaken, Hannah tried to calm herself. "Thanks for watching the kids," she said, realizing the need come across as meek and humble. Her mother was the only child care she had—and only because it was free.

"I'm blessed to still be alive," she whispered, "no thanks to my mother."

At least her sweetest treasures were safe, and she drew a satisfied breath of pride.

"Let's go home," she said out loud.

"Home," Matthew said, repeating her. His three-year-old voice was music to her ears.

Chapter Thirty-Three

Compromised

"Can you at least meet me half-way?" Jeremy was begging. "It's a long drive—three hours each way. That's six hours for me."

Hannah's teeth clenched in annoyance. "I—I don't know," she said, then took a deep breath and slowly exhaled.

Now she regretted answering the phone. Although her response had been swift, her words were still shaky.

"Oh, come on," he said. "Just this once. Give me a break."

Six hours *was* a long time to be on the road. "I—I'll need to think about it," she said.

She wasn't happy about this call, much less changing the kid's visitation schedule. In fact, she didn't want anything to do with Jeremy's visitation. She preferred he not be with the children at all. She feared for their safety. But her court documents clearly stated he was responsible for his time with them. And, she also assumed, financial and otherwise concerning his visits. For her, this arrangement was somewhat suitable.

"I don't have a penny to spare for gas," she said.

"Oh, come on," Jeremy said. "Work with me, won't you?" He was begging again. "The kids need to see me."

Why does he do this to me? Besides, he didn't spent time with them before. Why now?

Hannah took another ragged breath, then tried to stay calm.

"Tell you what," he said. "I'm a little strapped for

time. It's my week-end with the kids, but I have a meeting Friday after work"

"And..."

"If you'll meet me half-way, that's half the time for both of us, and could make things a lot easier."

"I don't know."

"Come on—for the kids."

"No."

"Give me a break."

Although she preferred saying, "Stop hounding me," instead "Okay, maybe," slipped from her tongue.

"I won't ask you again. I promise."

Yeah, I know all about your promises.

"You remember that gas station we used to stop at?"

"The big one?"

He cleared his throat. "Meet me there with the kids at 7:00 on Friday."

"What about my gas."

"I'll give you twenty to help you out."

"I'm not doing this again," she said, lips drawn. "I mean it."

"I just need your help this time."

She dropped the phone and then her anger exploded for being so gullible. He was playing her. He knew she wouldn't say no. The next instant she grabbed her head with both hands. *What if he brings a gun?*

"I'd better stick to my own guns next time," she said under her breath. She then inhaled deeply, realizing the ability to hold her ground was important for survival. She thought she was good at refusing Jeremy. But somehow, today she had failed her own test. "What if he kidnaps me? No one will know where I'm at."

She picked up the phone and punched in her mother's number. "Can you give me Fletcher's phone number?"

"Yes, Fletcher my cousin"

Having a nice looking man with her on the trip could be a good thing—especially if Jeremy got out of line.

Fletcher and Hannah soon settled in for the return trip home. The transition had gone well. Jeremy looked jealous until he learned the man with her was only a cousin. The kids then hopped in his car, and away they went.

But Hannah was dead tired. Mental fatigue was worse than physical. Now more than ready to go home, she relaxed and closed her eyes. The return ride would be less stressful. At least she was now home free.

Conversation with Fletcher was easy as most related to their growing up. But as the road leveled out, a hand lightly touched her leg. What was he doing? Still she didn't move. His touch may have been accidental, so she remained silent—eyes still closed.

The bantering continued a moment longer, but stopped when he squeezed her leg. This was no accident. Then, as a hand of velvet moved up her skirt, she instinctively recoiled.

"Stop. What are you doing?"

"You know you want it."

"Want what?" *How did I get in this predicament?*

The car then moved off the highway, and joined a dirt road. And Hannah grabbed her throat. A lump of fear was constricting it.

"Where are we going?"

"Just up the road a little way, so we can talk."

The car stopped, the ignition was cut, and he slid over beside her. "Just trying to help you out a little bit," he said.

"What—what do you mean?" she asked, brushing his hand off her leg. She didn't want to make him mad. He was her ride home. But, what did he think he was doing?

"Let's get in the back seat."

"Why?" She was stalling.

"So we can be together."

"No."

"All divorced women want it," he said. His words sounded effortless, but brought a new round of panic to Hannah's mind. But then he lifted her hand, and placed it on his expanding crouch. And instantly she removed it.

"You know you want it," he said.

"Not me," she said. "I'm not like that."

His arm tightened. "You know you want it," he said again. "You've been doing without. You know you need it."

"No, I don't."

But, she was stumped. What could she do?

"You know you want it," he said again, forcing his lips on hers. "We're kissing cousins, you know."

Would he rape her? What was he going to do?

"I'll—I'll tell your wife."

At those words he instantly dropped his hold, and bolted upright. "No. Please don't. Please don't tell her," he said, and looked distraught.

"I will if you don't stop."

Where had that idea come from? Hannah had to give God the credit.

The engine was again started, and the car was soon on the road.

Hannah took a gulp of air, straightened her skirt, and again stared out the window. But her hands remained gripped to keep them from shaking, and her heart continued to pound. She couldn't trust anyone. Not even her own flesh and blood.

Chapter Thirty-Four

Untrustworthy

"It's time for church," Hannah said; then opened the front door, and watched three mismatched youngsters march to the car. The drive would take approximately forty minutes.

Forty-minutes? Could she tolerate the bickering that long? But of course she could.

Their new church was a respite from the world outside—a haven in the midst of life's storm. Hannah believed this church to be the safest place on earth for her family.

Playing the piano for an absentee pianist then landed her a new position. And, as church organist, she loved every minute of church attendance. Devotion to God could now be spoken through music, and another way of worshiping him—the God who had delivered her from certain death.

Christian music was healing and therapeutic, and gave her purpose beyond parenting, and work. Perhaps the drive was a little long, but the reward was immeasurable. The children could now enjoy friends outside of their school and neighborhood. And, on many occasions, new friends squeezed in the car with them to attend VBS and other church activities. Yes, this was the life.

***

One Sunday evening, after the service began, a couple of visitors sitting in the corner of a church pew caught Hannah's eye, and a small gasp escaped her lips. The man and his wife were former pastor friends of Jeremy's. But should she go and speak with them, or just ignore them? Surely they knew she and Jeremy were getting divorced.

Later, following the benediction, Hannah made her way to the visitors. "How are you?" she asked, then extended a hand of welcome. "Do you remember me?"

"Yes, I remember you," the man said. "And I'll tell you this. You need to go back to your husband."

Aghast, and without a second thought, unrehearsed words fell from Hannah's lips. "What do you mean?" she asked. "He was abusive to me."

"I know he did some terrible things in the past, but you were wrong to leave him," the man said. His wife then nodded in agreement.

But, Hannah was stunned. *Could this woman also be a battered wife? And who are they to judge me?* At that moment she decided to never again subject herself to such nonsense.

Still stunned, she turned, walked away, and never looked back. Her mother was also adamant that she seek counseling, and then set up an appointment with her own church pastor.

"Once married, the Bible says you have to stay married—no matter what," the minister. "You need to go back to your husband, and pray he forgives you for leaving him."

"What is wrong with these people?" Hannah said out loud. "Do they want me dead?" It was again decided to trust no one, but her own instinct, and guidance from above. This alone would dictate what was true.

***

Later that week, as Hannah sat on the edge of the bed, a floodgate of memories began to release. Snippets of horror from the past again flooded her mind, and refused to go away.

"Austin needs a dentist," she once said to Jeremy

after tucking their son in bed.

"Kids don't need dentists," Jeremy said, then stepped into the bathroom. "

"He has cavities," Hannah said, following close, and twisting a strand of hair. *Dear God, please help him listen with his heart.*

"Baby teeth don't matter," he said; then reached for a toothbrush, and stroked his own pearly whites.

"Can't we at least find out from a dentist?"

"No." His words were cold.

"I really think he needs a dentist," she said. Now shaking, but determined, she plunged ahead; cringing all the while as she risked being pelted. "His baby teeth probably hurt."

"Kids don't need dentists until they get permanent teeth," Jeremy said, then slammed his own toothbrush in the holder. He then turned and faced her. "Why don't you shut up—you nagging bitch?"

"Please." Again she stepped closer. "He has cavities.

"I don't care. Now, get out of my way."

But when he shoved her through the door, she folded. Her hands were tied.

And now, shortly after their recent move, the children's new dentist reiterated the importance of having baby teeth repaired long before permanent ones were damaged. Hannah could only shutter at the pain Austin had endured. If only he had been to a dentist earlier. But, that was water under the bridge.

Chapter Thirty-Five

Ramshackle

The phone rang, Hannah stiffened, and her heartbeat instantly accelerated. *Why do I always do that?*

Had something happened to the kids? She had been on pins and needles the moment they left with Jeremy for the week-end. Were they hurt? Her lips went instantly dry as she grabbed the phone.

"Hello," she said, licking them. Still her voice squeaked.

"Hello."

The voice on the other end was quiet, and smooth. She had heard that voice before. Who was it?

Her forehead wrinkled in annoyance as she scanned her brain. Nobody outside of work, except her parents and best friend, had her phone number. Who was calling?

"Hello." Her voice was now a bit stronger.

"Just thought I'd see what you were up to."

It was him. It was Jeremy.

"How did you get my number?" she asked, voice cracking.

"Don't worry about it," he said. His voice, smooth and mellow, flowed strongly through the connection.

"How?" she asked, as hot air bubbled through her lips. "I need to know."

"I just wanted to talk to you—to hear your voice again."

"But I—I don't want to talk to you." Her words, although measured, were unfeeling.

"Please don't hang up." He was now begging.

"How did you get my number?"

"I have my ways."

No longer able to stand on legs of paste, Hannah flopped down on the nearest chair, and hugged herself. "Where are the kids?"

"They're fine," he said, and his throat cleared. "I just wanted to talk to you—."

"Let me speak to Haley."

"The kids are fine. They're with Mom right now."

"Then this conversation is over," she said, and tried to stand; but her legs refused to budge.

"Come on, Han."

"Please don't call me again," she said, then tapped her nails on the phone. "I don't want to talk to you."

"Come on, now. You know I want you back."

Her anger was now rising. "Don't call me again." But his words were causing her knees to buckle. Now unsteady, she stood to her feet, dropped the phone, and stumbled to the bathroom. Throwing up was on her mind.

How did he get my number? It was a secret. Did Mother give it to him? Did one of the kids tell him? How did he get it?

Hannah's head was now twirling in a crazy spin. He didn't want the kids this week-end. He wasn't even taking care of them. His mother was.

Again she dropped her head, and then embraced it. *At least I know they're safe with Grams. Him I don't trust.*

Again she lifted her head, and sighed. *I'll be glad when the kids get home.*

Her head was now throbbing so she stumbled to the kitchen, opened a bottle of Excedrin, and popped several tablets. But then she began pacing the floor—back and forth and back again.

"How did he find me? I didn't tell him. I didn't want him to have my recently changed phone number, or find out where we live. It's none of his business. He can pick the kids up at my parent's like he already does."

But as more panic surfaced, her heart continued to pound. Then, as a precaution, she stumbled to the door and checked the latch, making sure it was locked.

"He doesn't need to know anything about me—just when the kids are going to visit," she said out loud, then volunteered a half-laugh.

"Here I am, talking to myself again," she said.

Why did I answer that phone? What was I thinking? It's going to voicemail next time. I'm not talking to him unless it's about the kids per my attorney's advice.

Yes, that's exactly what Hannah would do from now on.

Chapter Thirty-Six

How Can I?

"Mama, I'm hungry."

Three starving innocents looked to Hannah for relief, and she didn't want to disappoint them. But, her heart was in shreds. What could she feed them? The cabinets were almost bare, her paycheck wasn't due until the end of the month, and child support, as expected, was again late.

Untold trials and tribulations were starting to pile up as she sat in the fetal position, head bent over. Frustration, lack of sleep, and constant worry was eating her alive. She was certainly feeling the pressure of single parenting, with no relief in sight.

How would she pay the electric bill? What would she feed the kids without money? And how could she drive to work on an empty tank?

At times her cries for mercy seemingly went unheard. Moist eyes, draining energy, despair, and desperation now held her bound. And, to keep hunger growls under control, her stomach was massaged.

But, she was tired of being hungry. Money was always tight, her paycheck spent long before it was received, and child support usually late. Her car was also falling apart, and the children needed clothes. Sometimes their tummies were empty too. *Help me, Lord. Please help me. I'm desperate.*

"What's the matter, Mama?"

Hannah lifted her head, not wanting her distress to show. The urge to give up was stifled, and she forged ahead. "Let's play a new game," she said, and a smile forced with emotions no longer felt. "Want to?"

"Okay, Mama."

"Go, and empty your piggy banks."

Three enraptured youngsters then scurried to separate containers, and returned with tiny assortments of nickels, dimes, and pennies.

"Austin, can I borrow seventy-five cents? I'll pay you back Friday when I get paid."

"Haley, have any birthday money I can borrow?"

"Matthew, got any pennies I can have?"

Small change, pieced together, bought milk and a few needed items; and seemed to fill the refrigerator.

"And what do we say when we pray?" Hannah asked.

"Thank God for piggy banks," Matthew said.

Giggles and muted laughter then erupted in the room.

***

"And thank God for store-brand flour and Crisco," Hannah whispered hours later. "Add a little water to the mix, and a dinner of biscuits and gravy is served."

How many times had she prepared this same meal for the children? "Fit for a king," she would say. And, they believed her.

What amazing food staples these two ingredients were. God was taking care of her family in ways seemingly impossible to others. Hannah couldn't help but recall a story in the Bible about a widow, and a prophet. All the widow had was a little oil and some meal. But as she prepared her last rations, she knew the next step for herself and her son was death. With no one to provide, they were helpless, and hopeless. But God sent a prophet to visit. Afterward her provisions stabilized, and they were able to eat during a time of great famine.

Exactly how many times had Hannah been like this widow woman? The times were too numerous to count.

Chapter Thirty-Seven

Christmas Basket

"Consider the ravens: they do not sow or reap, they have no storeroom or barn; yet God feeds them. And how much more valuable you are than birds" (Luke 12:24)

After placing the school's accounting ledger in the bottom of her desk, Hannah shut the drawer, and locked it. Next she straightened some paperwork scattered across the top, refilled the stapler with staples, and then slid three ink pens into a plastic holder.

"I'll be glad when today is over," she said in a whisper. "I'm ready for some off time."

The day was Thursday before Christmas, and she was anxious to spend some quality time with her children. Her new job as Office Manager in an optional school was enriching as well as enjoyable. Still, exhaustion following the stress of her recent separation was a constant issue. The responsibilities of single parenting were, at times, overwhelming.

Now ready to leave, she walked the short hall toward the side exit door. But then she spotted the janitor patching a square tile in the floor. She wiggled her fingers as a way of communication. "Bye, Clarence," she said "Hope you have a good Christmas. You're not working late are you?"

Clarence glanced up, and wiped the back of an ebony hand across a wrinkled brow. "As soon as I'm done with this floor," he said, "I'm out of here." But then he smiled. "Have a good one."

"Thanks, Clarence," she said. "You too."

She then turned, and continued walking toward the exit door. But when almost there she stopped one brief moment to examine new pieces of artwork created by the first graders and neatly taped on the exit side of the door. The festive creations of little students had captured the Christmas season in an assortment of color and design, and made her smile. But memories of past holidays brought instant tears, and she quickly turned away. She glanced around one last time, then opened the door, and stepped outside.

Cold wind hit her squarely in the face as she sprinted through the parking lot. She again glanced at her watch, and realized it was getting late. She pulled her wool jacket close; again breathing in the cold, frosty air. But at each excelled breath puffs of velvety clouds floated above her head, and wafted away through the frigid air.

The tips of her fingers were now numb as the bitter cold thrust freezing tentacles into everything around her. But after the door was unlocked, the rusty car ground and groaned in resistance as she squeezed inside. The corroded hinges then scraped together, and the door was quickly slammed—making sure it latched.

With a stiff hand she plunged an icy key into the ignition, and prayed the car would start. Black smoke with a charred odor then escaped through the hood, and she relaxed; then watched as it swirled into the wintery chill.

"At least the car started," she said to herself. "I'm sick and tired of this old engine huffing and puffing every time I turn the key.

Feelings of guilt then flooded her mind. "Please forgive me, Lord," she said. "I really am thankful I have a car—and it still runs."

But as embarrassing smoke continued to spout through the hood, she ducked; hoping no one would notice. The smell of burning oil would remain long after she drove through the small parking lot, and headed down the road. And yet, despite everything, she was glad to be on her own; free from the ravages of abuse, and a volatile man. In fact, she was happy to still be alive.

"Thank God the school bus has a route to my parent's house," she said out loud as the dated auto rambled down the road.

***

Once everyone was home, Hannah placed a small basket filled to the brim with various, but hidden, goodies on the kitchen table, and tried to stifle a giggle. Still she couldn't contain excitement.

"Look what my boss gave us for Christmas," she said, still grinning from ear to ear.

"Let me see, Mom," Austin said. He threw his kindergarten reading book on the sofa, and then sprinted to the table.

"Let me too," Matthew said, then rolled into a summersault on his way, squealing with excitement. Haley, slower than normal, shoved a second grade workbook into a worn red satchel, and then ambled to the table.

"I didn't see that basket in the car," she said. "Where was it?"

"In the trunk so you wouldn't, until we were home," Hannah said, laughing. Then her lips curved, revealing her excitement. "I wanted it to be a surprise."

Austin reached up and spun the basket around. "Let's see what's in it," he said.

"Looks like candy and cookies and some canned beans and stuff," Haley said. And instantly her eyes lit up.

"I want some candy—I want some candy," Matthew said, jumping up and down, and smacking his lips.

"Me too," Austin said, but glanced at Hannah for permission.

Haley eyed her mother again before lifting a small bag of red and green M&M's. "Can we have some?" she asked. "Please."

"Let's wait until after supper," Hannah said. "Then you can each have a hand full before bedtime."

"Thanks, Mama," she said, and again her face lit up.

"Oh, goody, goody," Matthew said, still bouncing up and down. "Let's hurry up and eat. I get all the red ones."

"Look," Haley said as her eyes scanned deeper inside the basket. "There's a canned ham in the bottom."

"I guess we'll save that for Christmas dinner," Hannah said, pleased with the notion that, at least on that day, their bellies would be full. Then, as if in a hurry, she placed three mismatched plates on the table.

"Aren't you eating, Mama?" Austin asked.

"I'm not hungry," she said. Her words, now scripted, were also automatic; and she held her stomach tight, praying the growls would stop.

Christmas Day would be special. For once Hannah's family would have a good meal to eat.

Chapter Thirty-Eight

No Condemnation

"Please, just leave me alone." Now more than annoyed, Hannah twirled a strand of already twisted hair, and then took a deep breath. "If you want to speak to the kids, say so. If not, I'm hanging up."

It was him again. And she hated when Jeremy called.

"Please don't," he said. "I'm begging you."

"Is this all you have to say?"

"I'm having it hard without you," he said.

"I'm hanging up now," Hannah said, and dropped the phone. Then she quickly walked away.

"Here I am—shaking again," she said out loud. "He makes me so mad. Why doesn't he just leave me alone?"

"Mom," Austin said. "It's ringing again."

"And, I'm not picking it up," she said. "Let it ring all night. I'm not answering."

Still Austin stood, as if waiting.

"He just says the same old things over and over again," Hannah said. "I'm sick of his begging. I'm sick of his intimidation. I'm sick of him."

"Was that daddy?"

"Yes, and I'm not talking to him. Do you want to talk to him?"

"No, not really," Austin said, looking sheepish.

"Okay then."

He went back to his toy cars, and Hannah put the phone on vibrate. Although tons of messages would remain to erase, at that moment she didn't care. Vile cursing and violent threats she could do without.

Still Jeremy's pattern had been in place way too long for her to think otherwise. After listening to many demeaning messages over the past several months, Hannah was learning to steer clear of his negativity. Humiliating words were hard to forget, and filled her mind with undeserved guilt.

In the past, his words had been pushed deep inside her heart. But now, if she could just erase them all—

Chapter Thirty-Nine

A Good Samaritan

In slow motion Hannah washed the supper dishes, but her mind was overburdened with the adversities of life. All she could do was to pray for strength to persevere. Her groceries had dwindled to half a pack of saltines, and a few scrapings of peanut butter in the jar. And, with that in mind, she turned and stared at the cabinets. What would she feed her hungry children the next few days?

Her paycheck wasn't due for three more days. Already her stomach growled from lack of nourishment. Still, doing without was worth the effort in order to live without harassment, and fear of retaliation from a sadistic husband.

A knock at the front door instantly jolted Hannah back to reality. Although the sound usually brought the children running, for some reason they remained in their rooms, and continued to play. But crash-night Friday was their night to stay up late, and they weren't in any hurry to give it up.

She peeked through the living room window, noting an overcast sky and the hazy silhouette of a lady about her age.

"Hi Ann," she said, recognizing a new friend who also lived in the apartment complex. "Why are you out so late? But come on in." In her friend's hand was a brown paper bag.

"No, I can't," Ann said, a tired look on her face. "I just came from the store, and brought you some food." Her face then lit up as she handed the sack to Hannah.

Tears instantly filled Hannah's eyes, but she blinked them away. "I can't take your food," she said, and tried to return the bag. But, Ann refused the offer.

"God told me to bring you this food," she said, and her words were firm.

"No, Ann. I can't take it. You don't have much either. Your family has needs too." And the bag was again thrust back.

But Ann stepped aside and folded her arms. "You're not taking her blessing away just because you won't take my food," she said.

Stunned, Hannah began to shake, and the contents of the bag began to settle. "I don't know what to say," she said.

"You don't have to say anything," Ann said, and then smiled.

"How did you know we were out of food?"

"God told me."

Again squeezing tears away, Hannah reached out, and grabbed her friend for a quick hug. "You don't know what this means to me—to us."

"I know you'd do the same for me," Ann said. "That's what friends are for." She then turned and walked back to her car. But as the vehicle pulled away, hope again filled Hannah's heart.

"Are not all ministering spirits, sent forth to minister for them who shall be heirs of salvation?" (Hebrews 1:14)

"Kids, come quick," Hannah said, "and see what God just did for us."

***

Several weeks later, after a long day at work, Hannah held up what looked like a book of stamps for her children to see. "Guess what I got today," she said, and waved the small packet back and forth.

"Let me see. Let me," Matthew said, and then reached for her hand. He tried to grab the booklet while shoving his sister's arm away.

"Mom, that's not fair," Haley said. "Make Matthew stop." But as oldest sibling, she wasn't about to let him beat her to the punch.

Austin, at the far end of the room, again glanced up from his homework, a smile of interest creeping out from behind closed lips.

"It's two books of Ronald MacDonald coupons," Hannah said. Her words were gushed. "Twenty dollars' worth."

She then twirled around, and did a little two-step. And immediately the kids joined her. And together they bounced around in excitement.

They never ate out—no money for extras, not even a candy bar or a Happy Meal to split between the three. They would use the coupons several times—stretch them as far as they would go. Hannah wouldn't eat—just pretended not to be hungry.

"How did you get the coupons, Mom?" Austin asked, now showing more interest.

"A representative from the fire department came to Hadley School today, gave a presentation, and then passed out coupon books to all the students." And again she lifted the booklets up in the air. "They gave me a couple of books too—just because I work there."

Then, as more excitement twinkled in the children's eyes, Hannah smiled even deeper on the inside.

"Can I hold them?" Matthew asked.

"Only one minute," Hannah said, then handed the coupons over. "But don't get them dirty."

Haley hovered near the doorway. "Mom, can we go to MacDonald's right now?"

Stalling, Hannah stared down at the floor, as if thinking. Yet it was so quiet they could have heard a penny drop—if there was one.

"In or out, sprout," she said, again laughing. "Last one to the car is a rotten egg."

Now more than jubilant, Hannah's heart did

summersaults as the joys of her life rushed past, bubbling with excitement. But once the car door opened, they scrambled to their seats faster than ever before; even buckling up without a reminder.

At least, for now, they could eat out like their friends, and not feel embarrassed, or out of place. God was still taking care of them—this time with coupons.

Chapter Forty

Undeserving

"How I wish I could find a house for us," Hannah said as she and her mother sat in the living room following work one afternoon. "We're tired of living in the apartment."

Then after a deep sigh, she continued. "Having our own yard would be so nice."

"Why don't you try and find one?" her mother asked.

"I've been looking, but there's no way I can afford one," Hannah said, then raked tired fingers through frazzled hair. "House rent is too high. Or, the house isn't in a good location. Besides, I'll never get a loan by myself."

"Why do you want to move?"

"Because, every time I get a raise at work, my apartment rent goes up. Somehow the government knows I'm making more money, and they take it."

"That's too bad," her mother said, still rocking back and forth.

"What about the house Aunt Jan owns?" Hannah asked. "When she passes, you're in line to inherit."

"The lawyer says it's tied up right now."

"But, it's empty," Hannah said, then clinched her hands together. "I thought you might let me live in the house so the kids would have a good neighborhood to play in, and I could get ahead on my bills.

"It may need be sold to pay her nursing home expenses."

"But, that may never happen. Besides, the house is just sitting there—empty."

"Well, you can't have it."

Hannah's legs instantly stiffened. "But couldn't I just move there for now?"

"No. If I end up with the house, I'm giving it to Bob."

"Bob? My cousin?"

"Yes, your cousin."

"Why him, and not me?" Air bubbles then shot through Hannah's mouth, and she blinked away new tears.

"He's the only person who helped your Aunt Jan. He fixed her heater, and did all her plumbing. If anyone gets the house, it should be him."

"But Bob already has a house," Hannah said, and new tears were wiped away. "He's established, and all his kids are grown."

"I don't care," her mother said, and then drew her lips into a firm line. "Like I said before, he deserves it."

Turning away, Hannah tried to swallow her pride. Without God's help she would never survive her nightmare of struggle.

Chapter Forty-One

Telephone Call

A pale pink envelope covered in a floral design was the only piece of mail in the box, and Hannah let out a long sigh. No child support today.

Now disappointed, she turned the envelope over, and noted Emily's return address in the left hand corner. *She never writes. I wonder why this time.*

Then, with a quick flick of the wrist, she ripped the envelope open; and a newspaper clipping dropped to the ground. But after picking it up, she released a gasp. A man had been arrested for killing his wife, cutting her body into separate parts, and leaving them in the trunk of her own car.

"But why would Now send this to me? Well, I guess she realized this could easily have been me."

Again she breathed a quick prayer of thanksgiving that it wasn't. She then turned, and walked back to the apartment. But once inside, the phone began to ring; and she inhaled quick gulps of air. How she hated that ringtone.

"That's probably Jeremy," she said out loud. But as far as she was concerned, their conversations were wasted. Although her attorney cautioned the need to talk when he called, she still dreaded the sound of his voice. Intimidation was the game he would play.

Past threats continued to haunt her. His promise to blow her brains out before their split still kept her focused, and frightened. The answering machine now retained many angry, menacing messages. Her life was still at risk. Only faith in God could keep her safe—and sane.

Although months of time had passed without incident following Hannah's separation from Jeremy, sounding relaxed on the phone was still imperative when he called. It was detrimental if he realized his ability to terrorize remained.

Her voice waivered, and then began to stabilize. "Hello?" To herself she sounded strong.

It was Jeremy.

"Hold on a sec," he said. Noises in the background then filtered through her ear after he placed his phone on a solid surface.

"I'm back," he said. "The delivery boy from Burger King was at the door."

"Okay," she said, blowing out some air. "What did you need to talk about?"

"Nothing really."

"If it's not about the kids, then I'm hanging up."

"Hold on a minute, will you? I just wanted to talk to you."

"Well, make it quick. I'm busy."

"You don't have to be so impatient," he said. But then the sound of munching grew louder.

"What's that noise?" she asked.

"Oh, just extra-large fries and a good old hamburger with all the fixings," he said. "Hold on a sec." And again the phone dropped.

He's making me hungry.

The next instant he was back. "Cheese was oozing out on the table, and I needed a napkin to wipe it up."

We're nearly starving here. Saltines and water for lunch today, and he can afford a meal—plus delivery?

"Hold on."

Again?

"He's wasting my time," she said under her breath.

Why am I even talking to him?

But his next words brought her back with a jolt. "I just wondered if you'd thought anything about us getting back together."

"No," she said. "Never going to happen."

"I promise. If we do, things will be different this time."

He's trying to ease his conscience.

"No," she said. "I need to go."

"Just think about it."

"Bye."

A sigh of instant relief filtered through Hannah's mouth. Still doing without was an easy price to pay for freedom. Even so, she wondered what the kids could eat that wouldn't clear the cabinets.

***

The next day Jeremy's words leaped out from the answering machine. And, Hannah didn't even hear the phone ring.

"It's your fault we're not together, you ugly motherfucking whore. You took everything important to me, and now I'm going to pay you back. You'll come out of work one day and I'll blow your brains out. I'll be in the bushes hiding, and you won't even know what hit you, you ugly bitch. You'll never make it on your own. You'll see you need me."

Silence.

"Come on—talk to me. Please."

The answering machine was full of recorded messages that crushed and mocked. Threats and coercion still sent chills up and down Hannah's spine each time she listened to Jeremy's new messages.

"When he stops ranting through the phone, I'll lift the receiver to my ear," she whispered.

Seconds later she lifted the phone. Despite the respite, she twisted the hem of her shirt in fear and annoyance. "Just leave me alone," she said. "If you want to speak to the kids, say so. If not, I'm hanging up."

"Please don't," he said. "I'm begging."

"Is this all you have to say?"

"I'm having a hard time without you."

"Doesn't sound like that to me."

"No-no. I only wanted to talk to you."

"Sounds like you're trying to kill me."

"No. You don't understand."

"Do you have anything good to say—anything about the kids?"

"No. I only wanted to talk about us."

"There *is* no us," she said. "I'm hanging up now." And, without a second thought, she dropped the phone, turned, and walked away.

"Here I am shaking again," she said out loud. "He makes me so mad. Why doesn't he just leave me alone?"

"Mom," Haley said. "I need some new shoes. These are falling apart."

The cheap pair Hannah had recently purchased for her at the dime store was now in shreds, and instantly her eyes filled with tears. But she brushed them away. She was doing the best she could. Money was always scarce. Pinching pennies was essential for survival.

"I know, honey," she said. "I need to buy new shoes for you, and Austin.

But I can't afford new shoes.

But, I don't have a choice.

But I'll have to charge them on my credit card.

But, I can't afford another bill.

Oh God, please help me.

Chapter Forty-Two

Insurance Failure

The mailbox was full to overflowing. Hannah, tears forming, stared at the box; then lifted the conglomerate. She let out a long, aggravated sigh. She then turned and, with a heavy heart, meandered back to the apartment; half afraid to examine the mix. In fact, she wasn't in any hurry to rearrange the bills just to pay the most important ones. So, without looking, she tossed the mail on a table and decided to tackle the pile later—after the kids were asleep.

Later that evening she quietly shuffled through the dreaded stack, placing the most recent bills on the bottom. Then she breathed a prayer that she would have enough money to pay what was due, plus food and gas. Thus began the tedious task of paying the monthly debt.

Each month, after Hannah's paycheck hit the bank, it was painstakingly doled out again. Utility vendors, apartment rent, car payment, and creditors were all hounding her for money. Ten dollars in quarters would cover their laundry expenses, and fifty would remain to buy groceries and gas for the month. Child support would fill in the gap—if and when it arrived.

The next instant a strange looking envelope in the stack caught Hannah's attention, and she paused. She studied the return address, then ripped the envelope open.

An invoice from Austin's last doctor's visit fell out, and the enclosed letter stated he was no longer covered under Jeremy's insurance plan. She was now responsible for the balance.

"What? Jeremy canceled the kid's insurance? Well, I'm not surprised." Ballistic anger then erupted, and Hannah put her hand over her mouth to mute her verbal rage. Still, her face flamed. Her anger was to the roof. Then, without thinking, she picked up the phone and punched in Jeremy's number.

There was no answer. But, she wasn't surprised. Again, she slammed the re-dial button.

"Hello."

"Why did you cancel the insurance on Austin?" Hannah's anger was coming through loud and clear—so strong she was shaking. "Did you cancel the other kids too?"

"Now, hold on a minute."

The voice on the other end was calm and collected, and she shivered in annoyance.

I think he enjoyed my outburst.

"What are you talking about?"

Her next words were spoken with baited breath. "I got a letter in the mail today stating that Austin isn't covered under your insurance. You are supposed to keep insurance on the kids. It's in our separation agreement."

"Well, now, don't get excited."

"Do they have insurance, or not?"

"Well, I dropped the family plan because you were on it."

"I don't need your insurance," Hannah said. "I have my own insurance through my job." Then she took a deep breath, and slowly released.

"Well, I didn't want to get stuck with your bills so I dropped the family plan."

"You're not being fair to the kids," she said. "They need insurance."

"Not my problem."

Slamming the phone down brought some relief.

"Our court-ordered separation requires he provide health insurance for our children," she said out loud." I guess this call puts all into perspective."

But how can I pay the children's medical bills from

an empty pocket?

It was time to add them to her own insurance plan. Despite the cost, the added premium would be money well spent.

Every day Hannah was fast learning to trust only in herself, as most around her were proving untrustworthy. And forget court orders. As far as she was concerned, they didn't exist. Right now was what mattered.

Again taking matters into her own hands, she could breathe a little easier. The children's health care was now in her hands, and not Jeremy's.

What other choice did she have?

"Absolutely none," she said out loud.

Chapter Forty-Three

The Price of Freedom

The sun was still shinning as Hannah re-visited her afternoon strategy. Starting today, the entire week-end was hers. And, she had plans. The children also had plans, and were on their way to visit Jeremy three hours away. Their Aunt Emily had volunteered to pick them up.

All were smiles as small arms waved and voices piped their good-byes. Suppressed tears then flowed, and usually long after they were out of sight. Always it was difficult letting them go. The vigor's of apartment life stopped the moment they walked out the door. But, for once, Hannah didn't have time to dwell on being lonely.

Spring was again in the air, and the aroma of roses, mixed with gardenia, gently filtered past her nose. A neighbor's freshly potted plants had earlier caught her attention, and she was anxious to see them up close.

She locked the apartment door, but stopped one brief moment to flavor the display. Still, she needed to hurry. The Blood Plasma Center would soon close for the week-end, and she needed to get there before it did.

A newspaper clipping, once carefully guarded in a zippered compartment of her purse, was now in her hands. The article, crisp and neat, again filled her heart with hope. Donate Plasma for Money. The ad—bold and provocative; the address—simple and direct.

Extra money in her pocket would mean more gas in the car, and perhaps enough to defray some upcoming summer expenses. The process also sounded simple, and not too painful.

"Short breaths," Hannah coached herself. "Take short breaths."

Later, as the hour was almost ended, her car sputtered up the rounded roadway toward a large brick building rising tall in the distance. The car then rolled into the parking lot, and Hannah scrambled out. The clock tower put the time at a quarter 'til five. She would need to hurry.

Once inside, a nurse took her pulse and other vitals, and her finger was pricked. Minutes later the nurse returned. "Honey, I'm sorry," she said, "but the iron level in your blood registers zero. We can't use it. The test says you're malnourished."

"Malnourished?"

But Hannah quickly rebounded. "Please," she said. "Test me again." And she wiped a tear away. "I—I really need the money."

"I'm sorry, but we can't use your blood this time."

Hannah's jaw again dropped, and instant weakness swayed her legs. All hopes were now crushed.

The nurse stopped one brief moment, as if concerned. "Eat plenty of green vegetables such as collard greens and broccoli," she said. "Build your iron. Then come back in a few months, and we'll test again."

Again blinking to hide her disappointment, Hannah hurried outside; wiping her face to mask the flow of tears. No iron? No wonder her hair was falling out by the handfuls, and her nails peeling; not to mention her always being hungry. Eating right really did matter.

Her ration of food was limited. Being frugal she always made sure the children ate first. If nothing was left, she got nothing. Only one paycheck a month, plus one from child support, and both needed to last until the end of the month.

Doing without was the only way Hannah's small family could survive.

***

A recent trip to Social Services was also a disaster in the making. But, Hannah was desperate. Summer was coming. And, as a ten-month employee, she was more than worried. How would she pay her bills during the summer months without a paycheck?

Yet she couldn't ask her parents. They had limited cash flow. And, pride kept her from asking the church. But after several sleepless nights she recalled several apartment friends who received government assistance. Maybe she should visit Social Services. After all, she did receive a discount on rent each month, due to low income.

Later, while waiting to speak with an agent, Hannah fidgeted with her purse, trying to stay calm. The children were tired, and driving her crazy from boredom. Not to mention chasing Matthew around the room while trying to keep him out of trouble.

She hated taking the children with her every time she went for an appointment. But, she had no choice. They were her responsibility, and she took it seriously.

Forty minutes later she was called to the desk. "Stay right here," she said, giving instructions to her brood. "Haley, make sure you watch your brothers."

Still worried, Hannah's heart pounded with anxiety. Leaving the children by themselves in a waiting room was always scary. But once in privacy room she gingerly sat down on the edge of a chair, folded her hands, and tried to remain calm. Then, as she waited, a hefty woman of color, quite rude in the scheme of things, shuffled through a stack of papers before giving her full attention.

"I need to apply for some sort of financial aid," Hannah said, when at last noticed.

"What kind of aid?" the woman asked in a voice that was crusty, and harsh.

"I'll be out of work this summer," Hannah said, rubbing her hands together. "I work for the school system."

"Do you have any other income?"

"Child support."

"In what amount?

"Four hundred. I have three children."

"How much do money do you make from work?"

Then, without saying a word, Hannah handed the woman a pay stub. Still the sound of fingers thumping stiff calculator keys made her nervous, and she stiffened.

"You don't qualify," the woman said. Her words sent chills up and down Hannah's spine.

Even if I'm out of work two months?"

"Your child support disqualifies you," the woman said.

"That doesn't make sense," Hannah said.

Silence.

Now crushed, Hannah slid deeper into the chair, and swallowed her pride. "I won't have enough money to pay rent and bills this summer," she said.

Still no response.

Perhaps standing would have more impact, but her legs refused to cooperate, so she again sank down in the chair. "How is it possible that I—I don't qualify?" she asked.

"We add all income together, and divide by twelve."

"But, I won't be working two months this summer," Hannah said, and her knees began to knock into each other. "Can we at least get food stamps those two months I'm not working?"

"You don't qualify," the woman said.

Again chills ran up and down Hannah's spine. *Why can't this hard-headed woman understand I'll have no money during the summer?*

Pangs of abandonment were again slapping her in the face. Should she take one more chance, and be bolder this time? Then she found her legs, and stood. "Please. I really need help."

The woman only frowned.

"Please."

"Next?"

The woman was dismissing her, so Hannah turned, and stumbled to the door. Still her shoulders sagged, as did her spirit. Defeat was written all over her face. How could she survive the summer with nothing but child support? It wouldn't be enough.

But she squared her shoulders, and stepped back into the waiting room where three rowdy kids were waiting.

Would this strangle-hold go on forever? And what on earth happened in there? Why did I even mention child support? "Well, because I'm an honest person."

Still she found it hard to understand how Nancy, one of her neighbors, and her two children qualified for food stamps, and she couldn't? Steak, potato chips, and colas were staples in their house, and purchased with food stamps. Would this insanity never end? Food stamps in her hands would purchase cheap meat, vegetables, and fruit.

Turning away, Hannah verbalized her thoughts. "I can't understand government logic," she said out loud. "I just don't understand."

***

Later, as Hannah left the blood plasma center, her heart was again fractured. Severe weakness was attacking her limbs, and her legs went numb beneath her. Yet somehow she dragged herself the rest of the way to the car. But once inside, she rubbed her head in frustration, trying to soothe the pain of hopelessness.

She was tired of the effort, and tied of the insanity. She was tired of working hard for little pay. She was tired of doing without just to survive. She was tired of everything— tired of it all. Surviving as a single mom was much harder than she ever thought it would be.

"Maybe I'll just end it all—right here and now," she said out loud. "Nobody cares. The kids will be okay—Grams will take care of them. And, they love her. But, how should I do it? Make the car go faster? Jump off a bridge? Take some pills?"

Ideas were coming fast and hard, causing Hannah's head to swim. No one cared if she died. Besides, she was tired of begging for scraps of food—tired of people looking down on her poverty—tired of struggling month to month. Simply said, she was just tired. What was the point?

Exhausted, and totally drained, she sucked in her breath; and closed her eyes. She now realized freedom had a price.

Chapter Forty-Four

Where's the Money?

The past few days Hannah had been more than worried. As a ten-month employee, her salary would end two weeks after the students were released for the summer. But Mrs. Foster, noting her despair, put in a word for her at the Central Office. And, at her recommendation, Hannah would be the summertime switchboard operator. At least cleaning toilets wasn't on the agenda, although any job would have been accepted with a smile on her face.

Her parents then promised to watch the children as daycare camps weren't an option. But the cost was harsh as punishment for misdeeds weren't optional, as far as her mother was concerned—and also part of her care giving. She often directed Hannah to re-punish if she felt the necessity.

But that notion was a constant noose around Hannah's neck, and she refused to deliver.

***

The following year Hannah was promoted to Administrative Office Manager at a local high school. Now a twelve-month employee, she could truly relax, and enjoy her work. Not only did full-time employment mean more benefits, but also more time on the job. Still, there was never enough money. The kids, now older, challenged the budget even more than ever before.

Making ends meet was still a struggle, and often fell short. There was never enough money for extras. Pinching pennies was still essential for survival.

But, Hannah was determined her children would have a good summer.

In the afternoons, and on week-ends, she learned that swings and slides at local parks were free. The public pool was also a great place to cool down, and reasonable if enough cash could be scraped together—plus gas for the car. The library, another option, provided free books, free movies, and other free programs. Signing the kids up for baseball and soccer was also worth scrounging for the fee. All three were worthy of at least that much.

They deserved a happy childhood, even if it cost everything she owned in the process. Besides, there wasn't anyone but her, and God, to depend on.

"He will provide," she often said.

The outdoor playground at East Library soon becomes their favorite pastime. After work she could rest on a bench while her restless brood exhausted themselves at play. Even the recreational area at Walnut Hill Apartments provided a turn-about glider. Great escapes didn't always require money.

Yes, Hannah could be creative if she had to.

***

The mailbox was empty—again—and Hannah wrung her hands in disbelief. "It's late as usual," she said out loud. "Eleven days past due, and still no child support. What am I going to do?"

But when she returned to the apartment, she again felt the heaviness of despair drop on her shoulders. What could she fix for dinner tonight? The cabinets were bare—two days now. But just in case she was wrong, she opened a cabinet door, and peered inside. An empty jar of peanut butter, already scraped and ready to toss, was the only item inside. "We're out of everything," she said out loud.

The children, hearing her stumble through the kitchen, ran up with the words "I'm hungry" on their lips.

"We're almost out of food," Hannah said, wiping her eyes. "Child support's late—again." And, she wanted to add, "as usual. " But instead she bit her tongue.

Still, bad-mouthing Jeremy was getting easier with each passing month. Yet she didn't want to sound harsh when speaking to the children about their dad. But was it wrong to say those things when they were true? Maybe the truth would be easier for the children to understand than half-truths. Besides, biting her tongue was making it raw. From now on, she would speak the truth. Whatever the circumstance, they needed to know just why there wasn't food in the house.

Her mind then shifted to her last conversation with Jeremy. "I haven't seen any child support yet," she said.

"Well, it's coming," he said. His words were spat. "I don't know why you're complaining. I need that money more than you do."

"How can you say such a thing?"

"You have a good job," he said. "You make good money. You know you do." But his words, smooth and confidant, had again slapped Hannah in the face.

"Not really," she said. "We're barely scraping by."

"Well, that's your fault," he said. "You left me, remember?"

Her face flamed as he continued his banter. But his words no longer moved her, as anger had long ago replaced that fear.

"I'm hanging the phone up now," she said, then walked to the center of the room, ready to drop the phone. But then she changed her mind. "I need to know when I'll have child support."

"With all that money I send, you're probably buying new clothes for yourself—new shoes, and things like that."

Still trying to stay composed, Hannah shifted the phone to the other ear; and then her thoughts were verbalized. "That money is for the kids—to help pay rent and buy food—for them—not me. I can live under a bridge. They can't."

"Yeah—right. You know you're spending all that money on yourself.

What a jerk.

This call is a waste of time," she said. "Good-bye." And, as a way of venting her emotions, she dropped the phone on the counter, and walked away.

***

School was scheduled to begin again in one week, and Hannah was concerned. She glanced at her feet, and then drew a sharp breath. The kids needed new shoes—all three of them.

Her thoughts then continued as she walked through the school parking lot to the car. Seconds later the vehicle rolled from the lot and headed up the road. It was time to pick her children up at their grandparents.

As for shoes, she had already learned the hard way— cheap ones didn't last. Maybe a good pair of sneakers would be worth the price. Yes, it would cost more up front. But shoes should last longer than six weeks—longer than the cheap stuff Jeremy once purchased for them. After the first wash Austin's clothes were handed down to Matthew. And, because everything shrunk, he and Haley both ended up with nothing.

But as the car rolled on, Hannah allowed a long sigh to escape. "What can I say to the kids?" she said out loud. Again, another sigh.

"It will break my budget if I buy shoes," she said. "I don't have money for shoes. If I buy three pair, it will take a whole year to pay off my credit card."

Again another sigh. "Oh well," she said. "The kids need shoes."

Seconds later the Honda rounded a curve, spun up the driveway, and stopped. Then, as she glanced out the window, the prides of her life, three bright-eyed youngsters, rushed out to greet her.

"Let's go, and buy new shoes," she said.

Squeals, shiny eyes, and glistening cheeks were all Hannah needed to realize she had made the right decision.

Chapter Forty-Five

Holiday Pause

"Hurry up," Hannah said, then jiggled the car keys. "It's time to go."

A blustery wind chilled her to the bone as she rushed her three children to the car. Haley, now twelve, and Austin, nine both climbed in the car and strapped in. A seatbelt strap was then found for Matthew, and he was also secured.

"I hope the car doesn't conk out," Hannah said under her breath as she sprinted to the driver's side. The engine was still thrusting billows of smoke from the hood each time it cranked. But the Honda was all she owned, so she breathed a quick prayer, and closed the door. Her prayer was answered. The car started.

The vehicle, now using a vast amount of oil, was a serious concern. Cans kept in the trunk were used daily to keep the engine from blowing. Still struggling financially, Hannah's new promise was making sure the children enjoyed their Christmas—at least as much as possible, despite the circumstances. So she plunged ahead with inner fortitude and blind faith in God.

Brenda, a co-worker, had earlier invited them to an indoor drama titled *Back to Jerusalem* at the Episcopal Church downtown. But with a serious lack of funds, Hannah was thankful the admission was free. If not, Brenda's invitation would have been declined. All she could afford these days were necessities.

But her children had long been anticipated this particular Saturday, two weeks before Christmas. Now bundled in undersized coats and assorted caps, they seemed oblivious to the harsh winter wind.

The cold more than accentuated the season as freezing air swept through the parking lot, and nuzzled at their ears. Inside, cold tiles on both floor and wall also enhanced the temperature as puffy breaths were exhaled and hands squeezed for warmth. Still, the excitement of the holiday made the wait tolerable.

Later, after a small intermit, Hannah and her three children followed a guide down the stairs, and into a huge basement redesigned as Jerusalem—all the way back to the time of Jesus' birth. Drama shop keepers selling wares on the street could be found in tents scattered throughout the city. A town crier then warned residents and visitors alike to register for a census in the town square.

Priests, dressed in traditional robes of the time, sold doves for sacrificial offering as chaos reigned. Other locals traveled on foot through straw-covered streets on their way to the center of town. Joseph, a weary looking man with a leather strap in his hand, walked beside an exhausted donkey. A pregnant woman hunched over the animal was tearful as the man asked again and again for a place to stay. Mary, his wife, was about to give birth.

The words, "No room—No room," were repeated again and again—some rudely, and some compassionate. But at last an inn keeper offered the couple a place to stay, in his humble stable. Mary and Joseph would share a stall with the few farm animals that he owned.

Straw was quickly arranged in the manger for a place to lay the new baby, and a bed of hay heaped in the corner would give Mary support during delivery. The animals could eat their fodder elsewhere in the barn.

Sincere reverence and calm serenity captured the essence of the season as Mary and Joseph, surrounded by shepherds and angels, proudly presented the newborn babe amid chaotic Jerusalem life. Jesus, the Redeemer had been born.

After the display, and beyond the manger scene,

Hannah stepped outside; and into the windblown sunshine. The children followed close behind. And although a snow flake or two cascaded through the squall, renewal beckoned them forward. At least the children now understood more clearly the true reason for the season.

Later, as Hannah's small family meandered to a camel staked near a tree, a beggar, part of the drama team, began asking for alms. Digging deep in the bottom of her purse, she prayed, through some miracle, that enough change could be found so each child would have a gift for the vagabond. Coins, however, could never replace the love this drama had instilled deep within their hearts.

***

Five days before Christmas, as her children acted out their own rendition of the birth of Christ with other youth in the church, the joy of the season seemed to explode. Still, Hannah was concerned. How could she possibly scrape together enough money from her meager earnings to make the final payments on her children's lay-away gifts?

Following the performance, presents under the church tree were shared. Fear and despair were then forgotten as Hannah's name was called again and again. Although undeserving, God's arms were still holding her close with reminders that his promise to never leave, nor forsake her, was solid.

Each child received a coat for the winter, and assorted toys. A brown paper bag full of goodies and fruit handed to each attendee was also embraced, and appreciated. But money given to spend only on herself is a legacy Hannah still holds dear to her heart.

Later after the program, with gifts in hand and a renewed faith in God, Hannah's family made their way home while singing the joyful carols of Christmas. On the way, a brilliant array of colorful lights displayed on homes throughout the neighborhood evoked a new sense of wellbeing in all of them.

Even a smoking car, with dents and peeling paint, couldn't destroy the thrill of the season.

This would certainly be a Christmas to remember

***

"For unto us a child is born, unto us a son is given: and the government shall be upon his shoulder: and his name shall be called Wonderful, Counselor, The mighty God, The everlasting Father, the Prince of Peace" (Isaiah 9:6)

Chapter Forty-Six

The Debate

Dating? Are you kidding? I don't think so.

Another man in Hannah's life was not a consideration. After all, she had all but been destroyed by one. But Pansy, an older lady in Hannah's church, was passionate about a newspaper dating service she had found. And, as a retired widow, she loved companionship, and often dated. She also lived at Walnut Hill Apartments, and was one of Hannah's neighbors.

A couple of months in a row she doggedly insisted Hannah try the service, assuring her the organization was authentic—a Christian organization that truly desired perfect matches for their clients. In fact, it was an original dating service for Christian singles. And when November's ads arrived in her mailbox, she eagerly shared them with friends. But, for some odd reason, Hannah was first on her list.

"Hi Pansy," Hannah said, after answering the door. "Come on in."

"You remember that dating service I told you about?" Pansy asked, after taking a seat. "I've decided to give you a couple of listings. Maybe you can find a young man to suit you."

"Thanks, Pansy," Hannah said, and tried to stifle a laugh. "But, I don't think I'm interested."

But Pansy only smiled back—as if defying her. "Take it anyway," she said, "and look it over. You just never know."

Later that same evening, after the kids were in bed, Hannah sat down on the sofa and flipped through several pages of available men—first names only—listed on thin sheets of paper. But the notion of another husband was quickly brushed aside. A few dates after her divorce only proved she wasn't interested in long term relationships. And yes, she was afraid.

***

The following month Pansy returned with a new list of bachelors from her mail-order list. Hannah scanned the names, and introductions were read, of available men looking for Christian companionship. The name Darren kept leaping off the page at her.

Darren. Why do I like that name so much?

But she laid the list aside for more pressing matters. The children needed her. And, after a couple of days, the list was forgotten.

Days later, when another week-end rolled around, she again scanned the list. "Darren" she said out loud. "A man named Darren. Maybe I'll write him a short letter, and see what happens."

***

The following Monday, as soon as Hannah stepped inside the apartment, the telephone rang. The kids, scrambling to be first inside, almost pushed her over. But she managed to grab the phone just before it stopped ringing. Still breathless, and quite winded, she quickly pushed her heels off and kicked them to the side. "Hello," she said, inhaling deeply.

"Is this Ms. Allen," a male voice asked.

Multiplied butterflies then flocked, and swarmed in Hannah's stomach. "Yes?" she asked. Her words were winded.

"I received your letter in the mail, and thought I'd give you a call."

"Who is this?"

"It's Darren."

"Oh." Again butterflies swarmed, but a hint of a smile shadowed Hannah's face.

"Your letter said you might be interested in getting to know me."

"You realize I have three kids, right?"

"Yes," he said, then cleared his throat, and laughed. "I'm okay with kids." And so the conversation began.

A week into January, following the Christmas holidays, Darren decided it was time for them to meet. A visit was planned—a blind date as it was—and the day marked in red on Hannah's calendar.

Chapter Forty-Seven

A Taste of Redemption

"I'll keep my date with Darren a secret," Hannah promised herself. "After all, this date is nothing more than a reason to get out of the apartment.

But sometimes I wish Jeremy would keep his visitation with the kids," she continued. "At least this week-end they have a birthday party to attend, and I can go on this date.

The timing couldn't be more perfect. Hannah's planned date with Darren would be at a Mexican restaurant close to the apartments. The children wouldn't even know she was away.

"Will he recognize me when we meet?" she whispered. "And how will I know him after only a few phone conversations, and a picture?"

Her thoughts then scattered as the phone's jarring ring set center stage. On the other end, Darren's explosive laugher was energizing, and catchy.

"It's a good thing I looked at a map last night," he said, "or I wouldn't be driving to Hendersonville today."

"Are you still coming?"

"I'm on the road right now," he said. "I thought you lived in Henderson. But when I looked at the map again, I knew I'd be leaving earlier. Hendersonville is quite a bit farther than Henderson. Remember, I live in Rocky Mount."

"Are you sure you still want to drive that far?" she asked, then held her breath, waiting for the answer.

"Sure I do," he said. "It's a long drive, but I want to meet you. Something keeps telling me I'll be glad I did."

He was coming after all, and Hannah danced around the table on her way to the closet.

Dressing for a blind date was electrifying, even though her nature was more tranquil than not. Then, after an uplifting prayer, her favorite perfume, used only for special occasions, was sprit-zed on arms and neck. Only then could she feel glamorous. Or, perhaps she was just happy getting out of the apartment, for once, without the kids. Whatever it is, everything just felt good.

And when Darren walked into the restaurant, shortly after her arrival, she knew exactly who he was. "I'm over here," she said, waving from a bench nearby.

***

The evening went better than planned. Still, Hannah was cautious, and somewhat anxious to check on her children.

After dinner, as she and Darren walked through the parking lot, the frigid January air hit them both squarely in the face.

She shivered a couple of times, and then moved closer to Darren. She linked her arm into his; not only for warmth, but to let him know she was happy. He then reached over, patted her on the same arm, and they both smiled. But on the inside she was giggling.

"Why don't you come by later after I put the kids in bed?" she asked. "Maybe we can talk more then."

Now, that was a bold thing to say.

Yet, in her heart of hearts, a gentle stirring of desire was beginning to surface. Was this more than just a chance meeting? Could this be a perfect match?

***

"Driving to see you every week-end is getting harder and harder to do," Darren said, and then smiled. "I'm on the road all the time now." He then reached out, and wrapped his arms around Hannah.

"You can stop any time you want," she said, blowing him a kiss.

"But, what if I don't want to?" he asked.

Laughter followed, and was sweet to her ears. The excitement of youthful anticipation then exploded in her heart.

"Maybe—maybe we should start making plans for our future," he said.

"Our future?"

He reached inside his pocket, pulled out a velvet box, and opened it. Bending down, he lifted a diamond ring in one hand while balancing from his knee. "Will you be my bride? Will you marry me?"

Overcome with both humor and excitement, Hannah reached for the ring, and slid it on her finger. "Is this a Valentine's Day present?" she asked.

"Well, it could be. What do you say?"

Tears instantly formed beneath closed lids, but on the outside she was smiling. "Yes, I'll marry you."

"I didn't think you would ever answer," he said, again standing. But he was grinning from ear to ear.

"I didn't think you'd ever ask."

He laughed, and then drew her close. "Well, we've only been dating a few months."

She smiled back, then pursed her lips for an invited kiss.

"Don't you really think it's too early to get engaged?" he asked, moments later.

"You're the one who brought the ring."

"I knew you wanted it."

"When should we get married?" Hannah asked.

"When do you want to?"

"Well, we're not getting any younger, you know."

"I think we're ready," he said, and placed another kiss

on her lips.

"I want a real wedding this time," she said, then drew a deep breath. "I eloped the first time—had a bad marriage afterwards. But, you already know that."

He smiled, and his eyes melted her heart.

"Will you move to Rocky Mount with me? Or should I find a job here?"

Hannah didn't need to think twice about the answer. "I don't want to up-root the kids from school, and their friends," she said. "Besides, I love my job."

"I don't have a problem moving," Darren said. "But, I need to find work before I do."

"Let's start praying," she said. "God can find the perfect job for you, right here in Hendersonville—or a town nearby."

"Make a list of companies," he said, "and I'll send out blind resumes."

"We need to pray over each one before you send them out," she said, and patted him on the knee.

"Agreed," he said. "That way, if I get a job here, we'll know for sure our plans are in God's will."

***

"Let's go ahead and plan the wedding," Hannah said, and placed an old Brides magazine on the coffee table.

"A long week-end will work best for me," Darren said.

"I want my kids in the wedding too," she said. "And, a pretty dress—a new one."

"I know you can't afford a new dress by yourself," he said. "Pick one out, and I'll pay for it."

"Really?" And she jumped up from the sofa, ready to give him a big hug. "I haven't purchased a new dress in a very long time."

"Whatever you want, you can have."

"No one has ever said that to me, and meant it," she whispered. "Dare I believe?"

Now energized, she plopped down on the sofa, and

started thumbing through a magazine. "I'll need to pick out some colors for the wedding."

"I think you need to pick out a day and a time first."

"I think you're right." And she giggled again.

Daren stood, reached over, and pulled the calendar off the table. "Here. Let's have a look."

"When is your next long week-end?" she asked, now staring at the calendar. "We could plan our wedding for that same week-end."

"Maybe you're right," he said; then paused and pointed at the calendar. "I have a week's vacation coming. It's the week of April fifteenth."

"Tax week?" Hannah couldn't help but laugh.

"How about tax day?" Darren's smile was unforgettable.

"That way we'll never forget our wedding anniversary," she said. And they both laughed.

***

The week of the wedding Hannah's telephone rang. It was Darren. "I just picked up the mail," he said. "A letter came in response to one of the blind resumes I mailed out. Gerber Baby Foods offered me a job, sight unseen. I have an interview with them in two days. They want to meet me, and verify my skills."

Hannah's phone instantly dropped, and she did a little Hallelujah dance around the table. But when she again picked the phone up, he was laughing.

"This job begins two weeks after the wedding."

"That's a miracle," she said, and tears began to run down her cheeks. "Nothing more than a miracle."

'You're the one who found the job."

"But you're the one who landed it."

"Our prayers worked," she said.

"This is a God-thing," he said.

"We're really happy together, aren't we?" she asked. But as more tears dropped on her cheeks, she dabbed them with her fingertips.

"You're the light of her life," he said. "There's nobody like my Hannah."

Chapter Forty-Eight

A Fairy Tale Comes True

Hannah felt like a princess in her new wedding gown. Well, not a gown exactly, but certainly a dress fit for nuptials—faded lilac lace with a fluffy white veil. A gorgeous pink, lilac, and white floral bouquet draped her arm, and finished the ensemble. Haley, dressed in flowing pink chiffon, was the flower girl. Austin and Matthew, both dressed in white slacks and pastel shirts, were groomsmen.

The small mountain church where Hannah retained membership was filled to capacity on the big day. Well-wishers, friends from work, and local church members were also in attendance. Even her parents came. Everyone seemed delighted she had, at last, found someone to care for her, and the children. Already Darren had been accepted in the fold, no questions asked.

At the bottom of the stairs, after the processional began, Hannah and Darren linked hands, and together strolled to the front of the church. A huge smile would then remain on her face the entire day.

"I've never seen you so happy," Darren whispered softly.

"It's the best day of my life, except when my kids were born," she said, whispering back. The minister's words then interrupted their undertones.

"We gather together here in the sight of God, and in the presence of these witnesses, to join together Hannah and Darren in holy matrimony. At this union they desire to enter into a sacred covenant with each other..."

With hands entwined, Darren and Hannah made their commitment. Then following a standing ovation, the congregants launched a loud cheer as soon as the couple were pronounced as married. Ecstasy swirled around the newlyweds as lips met for one deep and passionate moment.

Later, after the ceremony, guests headed downstairs to the fellowship area where balloons, ribbons, and pastel decorations were draped from ceiling to floor in springtime array. A three-layer white chiffon cake with eatable pink and lilac roses also awaited the couple's arrival. Then, as friends gathered near, the sweetness of their union was embraced, and celebrated.

Later, and still holding hands, Darren and Hannah slipped outside—ready to embark on their honeymoon as husband and wife. Darren's white sports car, decorated and inviting, now overflowed with streamers, confetti, and old tin cans.

Several guests followed the couple to the parking lot where more well-wishers were gathered to celebrate the nuptials. Clapping, whistling, and cat calling, loud and spontaneous, stopped them both dead in their tracks. Bird seed coming from every direction cascaded over clothing and hair; covering both from head to toe.

Once in the car they waved their good-byes through an open window as they huddled close in the front seat. Haley, Austin, and Matthew, arms bursting with streamers and silly string, laughingly urged them on their way. Their upcoming week was also a planned event. They would be the guests of a close church member, and their family of five.

Minutes later, as Darren's car rolled from the celebration, several vehicles followed close behind. Horns blasted, voices yelled, and tires screeched noisy congratulations as the couple drove from the parking lot. A conglomerate of old shoes, tin cans, and various trinkets jumbled, slapped, and clanged against their coupe in the warm April breeze as they headed to the beach for an exciting honeymoon retreat.

Their wedding, as later learned, had been the talk of the day.

Chapter Forty-Nine

Residual

The pain in Hannah's left side was excruciating, but she somehow managed to crawl to a chair. Then overcome with intense agony, she flopped down, and resigned to her fate.

"Hannah, honey, where are you?" Darren asked after coming through the door later that afternoon.

"In here," she said. Still overcome with pain, she had remained in the chair, unable to drag herself to bed.

"What happened?" he asked, running to her side.

"I don't know,' she said. "I left work because I was in too much pain. I'm still in pain. My left side is killing me."

Again holding her side, she tried to stand, but the pain was overwhelming; and she fell back into the chair.

"I'm taking you to the ER right now," Darren said. "Where are the kids?"

"They came home from school," she said. "I guess they're downstairs in the family room." Still dazed with pain, she squeezed her eyes tight. "I told them to stay close."

"Why didn't someone call me?"

"I tried, but the line was busy. I didn't try again. I was in too much pain."

"Kids," Darren said, his words resounding from the top of the stairs.

Haley instantly came running, and the boys followed close behind.

"I'm taking your mom to the hospital," he said. "She's sick. But why didn't one of you call me?"

Haley only looked dazed.

"It's okay," he said, not waiting for an answer. "Doesn't matter anyway."

He paused, and then said, "You guys stay inside. I'll give you a call when I find out what's wrong with your mom." His words, although hurried, were kind and gentle.

"Is she going to be okay?" Austin asked.

"Say a prayer for her," Darren said. "That's all we can do right now."

He then lifted Hannah from the chair, and helped her to the car. Her arms, although weak and exhausted, clung to him.

"Lock the door behind me," he told the kids. "I'll be home as soon as I can."

"At least they're old enough to stay by themselves," she said. "That's one less worry on my mind."

***

Once back at home, and Darren began preparing Hannah's medication after tucking her in bed.

"The doctor put your mom on pain pills after running some tests," he said when the kids came running. "If she doesn't get better in a couple of days, she goes back for exploratory surgery."

"I knew something was wrong when she wasn't in her office," Haley said. "The principal told me she got sick, and he sent her home."

"I tried to be quiet like she asked," Austin said.

"We just left her alone," Matthew said, bouncing around. "But, I got my homework done."

"Will she get better by Christmas?" Haley asked. "Remember, it's next week. We're out of school the next two weeks."

"I hope so," Darren said, then tousled Matthew's head. "Now get your baths, and your homework done. Tomorrow's another day."

***

The children were soon out of school for the holidays. But the pain in Hannah's side only increased in volume through the week, and she failed to enjoy the expressions of the season.

But early, the morning of Christmas Eve as she drifted in and out of sleep, severe pain encapsulated her body; and she awoke amid stabbing intervals of excessive throbs.

"Oh, God—it hurts too much," she said. "I can't wait any longer. My left side is killing me."

"What?"

"Darren. Call the doctor."

"But it's the middle of the night. Can it wait 'til morning?"

"No. It's killing me," she said. "Those pain pills aren't working. I think I'm dying."

Darren then jumped from bed, grabbed his pants and shirt, and hurried to the bathroom. "What about the kids?" he asked through the opened door.

"Call Mrs. Green next door. She won't mind checking on them."

Minutes later, and leaning on Darren's arm, Hannah was guided into the emergency room, where an attendant helped her into a wheel chair. The doctor was then called, and she was assigned a hospital bed. A gown for surgery was also donned, with Darren's help, and intravenous drugs started.

"I'm so ready for get this over with," she said. "The pain is horrible. It's killing me."

Darren's face looked worn, and his lips silently moved in prayer.

"I'll have my surgery today," she said. "Christmas will have to wait. And when I wake up, this pain will all be gone."

Minutes later, after the attendant rolled the gurney into the surgical arena, her thoughts rested.

***

Later, in recovery, Hannah's eyes blinked open, but felt weighted. Dozing on a chair beside her was Darren.

"I don't know why they always put Vaseline on a person's eyes during surgery," she whispered. "Maybe I'll ask—"

Darren's eyes then popped open, and he bolted upright. "You're awake," he said. "How do you feel?"

"Okay," she said. "I guess." But her words slurred.

"You sound like you're still asleep," he said. Then, reaching over, he brushed a few scraggly bangs from her forehead.

"I'm only half awake," she said, trying to laugh.

"I'm glad you're awake."

"What did the doctor say?" she asked, still blinking.

"You had the surgery. You're going to be okay."

"What did he take out?"

"Here's the doctor now," he said, then stepped aside.

The doctor moved closer. "How do you feel?" he asked.

"Drowsy," Hannah said. "I don't know. Better, I guess." Still her words were slurred, and sounded distant— even to herself

"I spoke with your husband earlier," he said. "Did he tell you about your surgery?"

"No, not yet. I guess this medication makes me sound funny."

"Actually, you're doing quite well considering the surgery you've just come through."

"What was wrong?"

"We removed your left ovary and residual scarring from Endometriosis. Then we cleaned the surrounding organs and tissue as much as possible. Your right ovary is perfect. No endometriosis found on that side. Only the left side of your organs were affected. Actually, your left ovary has been damaged for quite some time."

"Am I going to be okay?"

"Once you heal, you should be fine."

"Thanks for everything," she said.

"You'll have a scar from the surgery," he continued. "But as far as hormones are concerned, your right ovary will take over, and supply enough to keep you from taking replacements."

"That's good, right?"

"Yes, that's very good," he said; then stepped back, and reached for her chart. "Your incision was stapled. We'll remove the staples in about ten days." He closed the chart, and stepped back. "We can talk about that later. Any questions?"

"Why did I need this surgery?" she asked.

He paused, repositioned, and then looked directly at her; his pointer finger resting against his chin. "Let me ask you this," he said. "Is there any reason you can think of that would have caused your left ovary to burst open? I'm surprised there weren't problems before now."

The next instant she grimaced, and then grabbed her heart. Her eyes, although heavy, opened wide. "Oh my God" she said, and inhaled deeply. "It was Jeremy."

She took a deep breath, then looked at Darren. Still shocked, she blew dry air through already parched lips, and then squeezed her eyes tight. And instantly ruptured tears began to flow.

"That last beating, when Jeremy tried to beat me to death," she said. "He kicked me in my left side over and over again with his right foot."

Then, after a staggered breath, she continued. "My ovary may not have burst right then, but that's exactly what caused all this pain, and why I needed surgery. I think I would have died without it."

Chapter Fifty

Hospital Protocol

Later that same afternoon while recovering in the hospital, and after a nap, Hannah opened her eyes. "Is it Christmas yet?" she asked.

Darren smoothed her pillow, and then said. "Honey, tomorrow's Christmas day."

Surprised, she glanced at the doctor as he again wrote in her chart. "Can I go home today?" she asked.

"I wouldn't recommend it," he said.

"Please. My kids want me home for Christmas."

"Well—"

"My husband will take good care of me. I promise."

The doctor again eyed Darren. "I don't know," he said. "The hospital may be the best place for you right now. You just came through major surgery."

"Please. I'll do everything you say." Then she glanced at Darren, who looked concerned.

"You know what's best, Doc," he said.

"Please—" she was now pleading.

But the doctor only frowned.

"Please."

"Well—" and then he hesitated.

"I'll be good," she said. And her smile curved. "I promise."

Well, if you insist," he said. "Tomorrow *is* Christmas Day." He then closed the chart, and hooked it on the foot of the bed.

"You'll need to continue your pain medication," he

said, again glancing up. Then he turned to Darren. "Get her prescription filled today. It may be difficult finding a drug store that's open tomorrow."

"Then, I can go home for Christmas?"

He paused, placed his pen in a top pocket. "Only if I see you again—in my office—in five days," he said.

"I'll be there."

Again he turned to Darren, reached out, and they both shook hands. "I'll have my nurse give you an appointment card," he said.

"Thanks, Doc."

"See you Thursday then," he said, again looking at Hannah. He then smiled, turned, and headed toward the nurse's station at the far end of the hall.

***

Is it Christmas yet?" Hannah asked from a makeshift bed on the sofa two days later.

"Honey, yesterday was Christmas day," Darren said.

Shocked, she tried to sit up, but the pain was overbearing, and she cried out. Then she touched her side, and rubbed it gently. The staples felt rough to the touch.

"I should've stayed in the hospital longer," she said, again wiping tears of pain from her eyes. "My incision hurts."

"We tried to warn you," Darren said. "But, you wouldn't listen." And then he smiled.

"But, I wanted to be home for Christmas."

"Well, you were."

"And the kids?" she asked, pulling the afghan closer.

"Playing downstairs with their new toys," he said; then reached down and kissed her on the lips. "Where else would they be?"

She glanced at the corner trying to understand what day it was. Still confused, she watched the tree lights bounce off colorful ornaments, and cast beams of random color on the wall nearby. But as she watched, her eyes drew more tears.

"I can't believe I missed Christmas," she said. "I just can't believe it."

"Well, you did," Darren said, and then grinned.

"Did I even wake up once after coming home?" she asked. "I hardly even remember doing that."

But he only smiled, reached over, and touched her gently on the arm. "You were asleep most of the time," he said. "You ate some food a couple of times. Drank sips of water now and then. Other than that, you were out like a light."

"How did the Santa thing go?"

"The kids had a blast. Santa Claus was a very good man," he said, nodding his head up and down.

"Did they open all their presents?"

"What do you think?" And again he laughed.

"All of them?"

"You know they did."

"And, I missed it," she said. And another sigh escaped. "I missed everything."

"I took pictures and videos for you to watch," he said. "When you feel better, that is."

"I still can't believe I missed Christmas." And she wiped another tear away. "I've never missed even one."

Still overcome with sadness, she tried to pull up, but more pain erupted; and she again cried out. Darren then rushed over, and gently lifted her into a sitting position.

"It's time to rest now," he said. "Doctor Darren at your service." Then he grinned, and again kissed her on the forehead.

"I saved all your presents," he said, and then massaged her neck. "Don't rush, though. You've got all the time in the world to have your own little Christmas."

"At least I can watch Haley and Austin and Matthew's expressions when they watch me open them. That is, the gifts they gave me." And a giggle erupted. "I can't even talk straight. Must be the meds—making me sound crazy."

"You sound just fine."

Again she winced. "I'm still in lots of pain," she said. "But, I guess more from the stitches than the surgery. Well, it all hurts. What else can I say?"

Darren smiled, then glanced at his watch. "It's time for more medicine," he said. He turned, gaited to the kitchen, and then returned with a bottle of pills, and a cup of water.

"You'll get better," he said, and handed her a couple of pills. "Just take one day at a time. And listen to Doctor Darren. He knows."

Hannah snickered, and again grabbed her side to ease the pain. "Wearing one of your many hats again, huh? Lumberjack Darren, Plummer Darren, Mechanic Darren, Electrician Darren, Builder Darren, Darren the Toy Fixer. Who else?"

She laughed again, but then grabbed her side. "It hurts. Even when I laugh it hurts."

"Then, don't laugh," he said. "Just listen to Doctor Darren."

"You're the best doctor I've ever had," she said, and a smile flickered.

"I'm glad," he said. His face then contorted, and twisted into a grimace.

Still laughing, she held her side until the pain was unbearable.

"I've had lots of Christmases to remember," she said minutes later; again glancing at the tree. "But, I think this is the one I'll always remember."

"And, why is that?"

"Because—" and she wiped more tears away. "Because—I missed it."

Chapter Fifty-One

Unknown Visitor

A knock at the front door went unnoticed as commotion inside the ranch-style house was deafening. Austin's fourteenth birthday was in full swing, and several friends were bursting helium-filled balloons as fast as they could be blown up.

"Get the door," Hannah said, accentuating the word *door*. Still she continued slicing a huge ice-cream cake, but barely heard her own words above the racket in the room. But as the pounding continued, she yelled as loud as she could, "Somebody get the door."

"I'll get it," Matthew said. He slid off a wooden stool in the kitchen, licked his fork one last time, and promptly dropped it in a dish. He then sprinted to the door.

Once at the door, he stared through the peep hole, then turned back around—a funny expression on his face. He then sprinted back to the kitchen, knocking a chair over in the process.

"Hey, Mom," he said, panting. "There's some dude at the door." He turned, and again sprinted back to the helium-inspired group; looking for his brother.

"Hey, Austin," he said. "There's some dude at the door. Go and see if you know who it is."

Hannah again glanced through the door between the kitchen and the living room, as Austin gazed through the living room window.

"You know, I met that guy once" he said. "I didn't like him."

"Who is it?" she asked, stepping closer. But when no one answered, she glanced through the window herself. And instantly her heart began to pound as revolts of terror played havoc with her senses. *Why is Jeremy here? When was the last time we saw him—much less heard from him?*

Her hands shook with each beat of the heart as she opened the door. "I—I don't know what to say," she said, staring at Jeremy. Her words were forced. "Why didn't you call first? The kids haven't heard from you in—forever."

"I was driving through and wanted to wish Austin a happy birthday," he said. "Where is he?"

"Over there," she said, pointing.

"Hey, Austin—it's your dad," he said, and tossed a ten-dollar bill at him. "Don't you know who I am?"

Austin turned red. "Uh—no," he said. "Not really."

Still unable to move, Hannah stood to the side, and cowered. "I shouldn't be afraid," she whispered. "But, I am."

Now nervous, she straightened her shoulders, and then turned away. Things certainly hadn't changed much. But then she glanced back, and tears filled her eyes. Jeremy still knew how to wreck a perfectly good day.

***

Later that evening, after the remains of an active party disbanded, Hannah fell into Darren's arms; seeking comfort.

"It's okay," he said, holding her close. "Remember, I'll always be here to protect you. And, I'll always love you, no matter what."

Chapter Fifty-Two

Journaling

Hannah picked up a pen, said a quick prayer, and then reached for her journal.

It's been a long time since I've taken time to write. Still—

But since the kids are playing with their friends next door, maybe now is good time. If I jot things down, perhaps I can figure out exactly why Jeremy was able to control me the way he did all those years.

In the Beginning

Red, yellow, splotched and crunchy brown leaves slithered silently to the ground in the gentle breeze. But more leaves remained on several huge oaks and maples in the woods behind the house.

"I hate this time of year," she whispered. Again an agitated breath, and she released a very long sigh. "I'll be raking leaves 'til June."

Her seven-year-old eyes squeezed tight as she tried to stop the flow of tears. "But if I don't keep raking, I'll be very, very, very sorry."

Raised whelps on legs and arms were still stinging, and she groaned in agony. Punishment was always harsh. Would it always be this way?

Broken Song

A basket of freshly gathered eggs was on its way to the basement for processing as her eleven-year-old voice filtered through the air in melodious refrain. New and made-up words then erupted as she meandered toward the basement, the handle of a yellow basket held tightly in her hand. Six hundred or more chickens could lay dozens in one day. Still, gathering eggs was only one of many chores assigned to her, and an everyday requirement.

The next instant she tripped, and then landed on the hardened ground. The eggs in her basket instantly scattered around her. The container, still tilted, was now upside down.

Now panicked, she gathered the unbroken eggs, one at a time. Several were cracked, and a couple oozed a sticky, yellow gob on the ground. But, she needed to hurry. Her father, in the distance, was coming toward her.

"Look at all these broken eggs," he said. But his words were harsh, and she cowered. "Why did you break them?"

"I—I tripped and fell," she said, wincing. Her scraped knee was now bleeding, and screamed for attention. But it was ignored because she was afraid.

"Pick these eggs up," he said. "You'll pay for every one that's broken. I can't afford broken eggs."

"I didn't mean to fall," she said, a tear in her eye. But as her bloodied knee continued to throb, she reached down to rub it.

"I don't know why I tripped," she said, and then looked up.

"It costs me money when you break an egg," he said. Still, the look on his face, and the tone in his voice, made her shudder; and she turned away.

"Count all these broken eggs," he said. "You'll pay me for every single one that's broken."

She didn't have any money. Well, her birthday money, but it wasn't much.

She could only pray it was enough

The Unspoken

A lifetime of experience had taught her mother's command required immediate compliance.

"Now, you listen here," she would say. "Get me a switch."

But was forgetting to wash a couple of cooking pots so terrible? The stove, counter, and tabletop had been full of dirty dishes. How did she miss those pots?

Already scrubbed dishes had been stacked in the cabinet before the greasy, crusty pans were tackled. Dried food plastered over every inch of porcelain had been difficult to scrub.

Again she glanced at her mother, then scrambled to the tree used for switches. The branch needed to be long enough, and thick enough. Even better would be new sprigs growing on the stick. The switch needed to please her mother, or she would be lashed twice as long. But this wasn't the first time she had been in trouble. And, it surely wouldn't be the last.

Still searching for a perfect switch, she visualized many throbbing stings that would last a few minutes, and probably bring blood. But, sometimes, the scars would remain for weeks.

Her teachers never asked about the scratches and scabs on her legs. But they must notice, because all she ever wore is a dress.

The tree branch, now pre-tested to make sure her mother was please, was selected. But she didn't want another beating. She only wanted to finish the dishes so she could read her new library book.

She loved to read. But what else was there to do when a spare minute surfaced? No television, no radio, no phone—wasn't allowed to go anywhere but school, and church.

Reading was a fantasy world for her, as household duties, and work on the farm, took most of her time when not at school, or at church. But responsibilities at home often stretched her energy. She was, after all, just a child.

She handed the stick to her mother, and then cowered; preparing for what was ahead—a good whipping.

But the sternness on her mother's face, no matter the reason, was enough to make her push the panic button. Internalized fear then arose in her chest, and her heart pounded in chunks of dread.

"You stand right there while I whip you" her mother said. Her words brought instant compliance.

And instantly the arm lifted, and the branch came down on her legs. She tried not to jump as the switch descended again and again, covering her legs, torso, and arms with whelps and blood.

The next instant she bit her lip and tried not to cry out as silent tears oozed from her eyes. The strokes were merciless and harsh.

But, that's just the way it was.

***

Oh, God. Please help me. How can I continue to write? My childhood memories are tearing me apart.

Why have I never before realized the role my parents played in the decisions I've made over the years. And now—

But, revelation is truth. And truth is revelation. With pen in hand, Hannah's journaling continued.

Responsibility

Her father took a final sip from his coffee mug, and then looked at her. "It's time to go," he said. "You ready?" He then pushed his chair back under the table, and stepped away.

"Make sure you keep a record of your rides," he said."
You can pay me when you get paid."

"Does this mean per day, or per trip?" she asked.

"Every trip. That's two a day."

"Like a taxi cab?"

"Yes—like a cab."

Her eyelids, still heavy with sleep, drooped as she squinted in the pale moonlight. At 5:00 in the morning, her internal clock screamed for more sleep. But, she needed to wake up. If she didn't, she would surely be in trouble.

Her eyelids again stretched, and she choked back a yawn. *I don't know how to be a waitress. I guess someone will teach me.*

Again, another yawn.

Why did Mother get me this job? Well, she said I could buy the clothes I needed. And shoes. Maybe she'll let me buy some shampoo too.

Later, as the truck rolled through a rock gate, she pulled her thin sweater close. But in her head she tried to prepare for what was ahead. *What if nobody likes me? And what if I'm the only kid who works there?*

The truck rolled up to the cafeteria entrance, the break was applied, and the engine stopped running. "Remember, I get off at two," she said, and waited for a response.

"I'll be here when I get here," he said. "Did you tell your mother what time?"

"She'll remind you."

Still she remained frightened. Never before had she worked in a public place. But, at least for now, she could buy some new shoes after she was paid. Her old ones were scruffy. New shoes would be nice.

A worker's permit in hand, she opened the cafeteria door; and stepped inside. Still her hands trembled, and she broke out in a sweat. But after a raspy breath, she glanced around; looking for Mrs. Osteen, her new boss.

Getting a worker's permit as a thirteen year-old, her

mother by her side, had been easier than going inside this century-old building alone.

Blue Shoes

She pulled a thin gray cardigan—now one size too small—over her head, and headed out the door. In her hand was a small purse where a few dollars had been tucked. Martin's, a local shoe store in her home town, was the destination.

On the inside her heart pounded with excitement. Today she would replace her scruffy worn-out shoes with a brand new pair. Her scrunched-up toes had long screamed to escape their cramped confinement. And, today was the day.

Her father's old truck rattled in the wind as they bounced along. The outside air was chilly, and she rubbed her hands together, trying to stimulate some warmth. Air in the compacted cab was nippy as the heater had long before stopped working. Each accelerated breath now collided with the cold; creating tiny cloud puffs that gently wafted away in the frigid air. Winter could be harsh in their small mountain town.

A polished array of new shoes in the window display at Martins shimmered beneath brilliant white lights. Still her heart pounded as she stepped through the small store entrance. But then she stopped one brief moment, and glanced out the window. Far in the distance she could see her father's truck as it drifted out of sight. He needed a couple of tools from the hardware, so she would be shopping alone.

Then, after a quick breath to calm herself, she skipped to the center isle where the warmth of vented air enveloped her face. Muted blue brogans with elastic slits on the side then caught her attention. They looked sturdy, and quite stylish. Besides, she loved blue.

The shoes were a perfect fit. With tote in hand, she again stepped outside to wait on her father. The blustery wind then caught the hem of her sweater as she waited, and flapped it hard against her face. But she brushed it away, and hunched over; trying to stay warm—the shoe box encased tightly in her arms. Minutes later the truck rattled to the curb, and she climbed inside.

"I need to run by the Johnston's on the way home," her father said as they pulled away.

As they bounced along, she stared at the hood over the truck engine, and tried to entertain herself. Peeling paint of different levels left the impression of maps in her head, and she smiled. Meanwhile, her father's whistling echoed through the cab. But when the song ended, they rode along in silence.

Her new purchase was now calling her name, so she looked down, and stared long and hard at the package in her lap. Then, in contentment, she drew a heart-felt breath. She then peeled the box open, and stared down at the contents.

What beautiful shoes they were—muted blue resting on a crumpled bed of tissue white. "I love my new shoes," she said. "I can't wait to wear them to school."

Minutes later the truck rolled into the Johnston's drive, and her father climbed out. "You can play with those kids over there," he said, pointing. "That is, if you want to."

She followed the direction of his finger, and noted a group of children playing with a yellow ball.

"Stay close," he warned. "I'll only be a few."

She covered her new brogans with the tissue, closed the box, and then shoved all in the glove compartment. Now confident her shoes would be safe, she jumped down from the step bar to the ground. The door then slammed, and she looked across the way at a short girl in a pink jacket. The girl was waving for her to come over.

Later, when motioned back, she ran to the truck. Now hot, sweaty, and out of breath from her run to the truck, she climbed in; leaving the door to swing closed behind her.

Once home she breathed a long sigh of relief.

"Where are your new shoes?" her mother asked, a smile on her face.

"Oh," she said. "They're still in the truck," and then raced back to get them. She jerked the glove box open, and instantly let out a gasp. Her new shoes were gone. But she was positive she had left them in the compartment. Where were they?

A knot of dread was now creeping up her throat as she reached under the seat, scrambling in her haste to find the lost box. Each side of the seat was then explored. Every nook and cranny was searched until her fingers were stiff and numb. But, her new shoes were non-existent—gone without a trace.

She inhaled another deep breath, then ran back to the house. Still running, she called for her mother. "I can't find my new shoes," she said. "They're gone. I can't find them."

Her mother's face fell. "What happened?"

Tears again filled her eyes and slid down her cheeks. "I left them in the glove compartment of the truck—like daddy said."

Another staggered breath.

"Some kids wanted me to play when he stopped at the Johnston's."

"Was the truck locked?"

"I don't know. I think so."

"You know we can't buy you another pair," her father said as he walked across the floor. "You should have taken better care of those shoes."

"I didn't know they would get gone," she said. Then new tears formed, and ran silently down her cheeks.

But he only turned, and walked away.

Later that same afternoon, as she sat on the porch step alone, she scrunched up her eyes and tried to understand what had happened to her new shoes.

"There's always a reason things happen," she said, nodding her head up and down. She then lifted the hem of her dress, dried her eyes, and looked down at her scruffy browns. "I'll polish them one more time, and hope they don't look too ratty."

Another sigh escaped.

"I didn't see anyone near the truck at the Johnsons," she said to herself. "But, I was busy chasing that old yellow ball." *How did my shoes disappear?*

Her shoulders slumped as she resigned to her fate.

"It's not my fault those shoes got gone," she said in low tones. "But I shouldn't be too upset."

Then, in gesture of surrender, she turned both hands up. "After all," she said, "they're just shoes. Someone must have needed them more than I did."

Unfair

"If you ever shave your legs, you'll get the biggest whipping you've ever had."

Her mother's words were to be reverenced. She always meant exactly what she said. A lifetime of beatings had, long ago, made her a believer.

But surely her sixteenth birthday would to be a turning point. Maybe, just maybe, her mother would let her shave them, like the other girls. Goodness knows, she had begged long enough; even asked Ruth, a cousin, to rally for her. But that didn't work either. And, because she would never disobey, she was stuck.

So, until she received her mother's blessing, they would remain unshaven, and she would continue being taunted at school. Yet her mother would surly know if she disobeyed because her legs were checked every day—just to make sure.

***

A Cry for Help

How she dreaded making this call. But, there wasn't any other choice.

"Mother, my car broke down," she said. "Can you get daddy to come and get me?"

"Where are you?"

"About an hour away."

"Hold on." The noises in the background then increased after her mother dropped the phone. Minutes later it lifted. "He said it's too far, and he needs his rest."

She wasn't surprised. Yet she felt uneasy. Being alone was scary, even as a young adult.

"It's getting dark, and the station will close in a couple of hours," she said to her mother.

Still on the phone, she glanced around the small enclosure; and noticed a group of strange men huddled together on the outside. Fear then gripped her by the throat. Braving a three-hour trip alone had been overwhelming. But the need to get away from Jeremy for a breather was essential. Visiting her parents provided the excuse.

"I'll see if your cousin can drive down and get you," her mother said.

"Okay. But let me know if he can. In the meantime I'll see when the car can be fixed."

At least her cousin cared. Yet she didn't have much to depend on—certainly not Jeremy, or her own father. Neither cared if she was stranded, or not.

The truth stung.

***

The week-end was almost over, and she was glad. Spending time with her parents had revealed serious drawbacks. Boredom and inactivity was to blame.

She placed the phone on the table, then straightened her back, and rubbed her head. "That was my mother-in-law," she said. "She and Waine, Jeremy's brother, are driving down to get me. We'll pick my car up on the way back."

"How nice of them to drive all that way," Mother said yet continued to rock in her chair. "When are they coming?"

"Tomorrow morning. They plan to leave early—should be here before noon."

"What did the station say about your car?"

"The starter's been replaced, and tested. It runs fine now."

'Well, that's good," her mother said, then reached for a knitting basket beside the chair.

"What are you making?" she asked, trying to sound interested.

"Slippers," her mother said, still rocking. "I'm knitting all my friends at Sunday school a pair for Christmas."

"That's nice. Pretty color too."

"I hope they like them."

Her return smile was forced. "I think I'll go and pack my stuff," she said. "Tomorrow will be here before I know it."

She now realized, living with Jeremy, as bad as it was, was better than visiting her parents.

***

The world outside was wet—washed clean by a recent thunderstorm as a brown sedan pulled up the drive. Mrs. Allen then climbed out, and gave her a big hug.

"Thanks for coming to get me," she said.

"Gives me and Wayne a chance to see the mountains again," Mrs. Allen said, then waved at her mother on the porch.

"Wayne—how did your new car climb the mountain?"

"Pretty good," he said. "But, that mountain is steep for a car. No wonder yours conked out."

She reached over and patted him on the shoulder. "I

wasn't on the mountain," she said. "My car is on the other side, an hour back."

He only laughed.

"Anyway, thanks for coming to get me."

"Didn't want to leave you stranded," he said, and then chuckled.

***

Hannah closed the journal, and then wiped her swollen eyes. A new box of tissues beside her was now empty.

What good is it now to realize that the people in my life, who should have cared the most, didn't?

That lack of support has all but stifled the life out of me, and caused me to accept the unacceptable.

She winced, blinked her eyes, and then took a deep cleansing breath as new wisdom took center stage.

Chapter Fifty-Three

Resignation

After handing a ticket to the flight attendant, Hannah stepped aboard the jet, and found her seat. Flying to Hendersonville for a previously scheduled court appearance was on the agenda.

Darren was now employed by Wesson Oil, a prominent company located in Savannah, Georgia. Austin, sixteen, and Matthew, fourteen, were both part of the moving entourage. Haley, recently graduated, had decided to launch out on her own, and would remained in the mountains of western North Carolina.

The rigors of chasing an ex-husband for child support over the years had been exhausting. His support, over time, had dwindled to nothing. Darren's provision, however, far outweighed what would have been Jeremy's supplement. Still Hannah wanted Jeremy to feel the pressure of compliance once again, and had decided to try and collect back child support, while requesting the court's approval for future funding. And, because the appointment was in place before the move, she was determined to keep it.

An hour later, after the plane landed, she swallowed her fear, and then climbed down narrow metal steps onto the tarmac. But once disengaged, the effects of mountain breezes and cooler temperatures seemed to quiet her inner turmoil. She was now ready for the challenge

Tuesday arrived and, once again, she climbed the marble courthouse steps. But her head started to pound as fear again surfaced. Yet she wasn't surprised. Always, when

Jeremy was in a room, she was afraid.

However, less than an hour later, she was again down the stairs. He was a no-show.

At first she was surprised, but, in reality, wasn't. At that moment she decided to never again pursue him for child support. As far as she was concerned, he had won the battle. Child support was nice, and once desperately needed. But a faithful, loving husband was much better. Darren's role as father-figure would continue with or without child support from Jeremy.

It came as no surprise how easily Jeremy had fallen in line with other delinquent dads. His true character was still shining through.

The following day she boarded a return flight to Savannah. Although short in duration, this trip had resulted in understanding, resignation, and acceptance.

The following year, Hannah and her family were living in Dallas. Darren's employer, after closing the Savannah plant, had moved them to the big state of Texas.

Chapter Fifty-Four

Covenant of Peace

Although divorced several years from Jeremy, Hannah still faced severe difficulties in relinquishing past hurts.

One morning, after she opened the Bible, words of consolation found in the book of Isaiah leaped off the page, and into her heart. This portion of scripture was, without a doubt, a direct word from God to her.

"Do not fear, for you will not be ashamed; neither be disgraced, for you will not be put to shame. **For you will forget** the shame of your youth, and will not remember the reproach of your widowhood (separation, divorce) anymore.

For your Maker is your husband, The LORD of hosts is his name; and your Redeemer is the Holy One of Israel; He is called the God of the whole earth.

For the LORD has called you like **a woman forsaken and grieved in spirit; like a youthful wife when you were refused**," says your God. "For a mere moment I have forsaken you, but with great mercies I will gather you. With a little wrath I hid my face from you for a moment; but with everlasting kindness I will have mercy on you," says the Lord your Redeemer.

"Oh you afflicted one, tossed with tempest, and not comforted. Behold, I will lay your stones with colorful gems, and lay your foundations with sapphires.

I will make your pinnacles of rubies, your gates of crystal, and all your walls of precious stones. All your children shall be taught by the LORD, **and great shall be the peace** of your children. In righteousness you shall be established. You shall be far from oppression, for you shall not fear; and from terror, for it shall not come near you.

Indeed they shall surely assemble, but not because of Me. **Whoever assembles against you shall fall for your sake...**

No weapon formed against you shall prosper and every tongue which rises against you in judgment you shall condemn.

This is the heritage of the servants of the LORD, and their righteousness is from me," says the LORD" (Isaiah 54:4-17)

***

In an instant, years of anguish were let go as tears of release splattered the open page. Revelations of her dark past had been revealed, and Hannah could now heal from the pain of the past.

Chapter Fifty-Five

Deathbed

Texas summers can be brutal—the heat often unbearable for those on the outside. "Thank God for air conditioners," Hannah said, after the phone disconnected. But on the other end, Haley's shared information had been somewhat unnerving.

"Austin—Matthew," Hannah said, urging her sons, then nineteen and seventeen, into the family room. "It's time for a family conference."

But when the two gathered near, she spoke in soft undertones. "Hey guys—listen," she said, moving closer. "I just talked with your sister. Your real dad isn't doing so well." Then, feeling weak, she pulled out a chair, and sat down. "Actually, he's on his deathbed."

"What?" Their startled response then echoed through the room.

"You knew he was diagnosed with cancer. Three cancers to be exact."

"Yeah, I knew," Matthew said. "So what?"

"Well, he's dying," Hannah said; then twisted around and looked closer at them.

"When?" Austin asked, then stood in silence, taking it all in.

"Nobody knows, really," she said. "Probably soon."

Matthew grinned, then plopped down on a chair beside her, and fingered a cushion. "So, why did you call them in here?" he asked.

"Darren and I think you two, and Haley, need to see

him before he passes," she said. "What do you think?"

Matthew reached over, picked up a loose CD, and began twirling in though his fingers. "When?" he asked.

"We thought we'd get tickets and fly from DFW to Hendersonville. Haley said she could drive everyone in her car to see your dad."

Matthew, still twirling the disc, sat in silence.

"Austin, you and Matthew can ride with her."

"Huh? Oh, okay," Matthew said; then stopped his twirling, and glanced up. "When?"

"Next Wednesday. We'll stay until Saturday. You're out of school a couple of days, so you won't have any make-up work. Austin, you need to tell your boss that you can't work those days, and your teachers at college."

"Aren't you going with us?" Austin asked, looking concerned.

"Only to Hendersonville," she said. "And since Haley lives there, the transition will be easy."

Still uneasy, she tried to stand, but quickly sat back down. Her knees were buckling.

"Why should we go?" Matthew asked.

"Because—I think you need to see him. He's dying. I know he's never been much to you, but—he is your natural father."

Austin glanced away, inhaled some air, and then slowly released. "Okay—I guess," he said.

"At least we get to fly most of the way," Matthew said. He stood, and then romped to the door, still twirling the disc.

***

Beads of sweat popped out on Hannah's forehead after her children came into the room. "How did it go?" she asked, after sitting down.

"Dad was glad to see them," Haley said, smiling. "He hugged us all."

Matthew grinned, and then plopped down on the sofa

beside Hannah. "He was in bed the whole time," he said, before throwing a pillow at his brother.

"He looked really skinny," Austin said, then ran his hand through his own thick mane. "All his hair was gone, and everything."

"Aren't you glad you went to see him?

"Yeah, I guess so," he said.

"How did his new wife treat you?" Hannah asked.

"She wasn't too friendly," Haley said. "I don't think she liked us being there."

"He never got out of bed," Matthew said. "Not even once. But, I didn't really remember him from before."

"Did he give you anything?" Again, Hannah couldn't help but ask.

"Uh, well, not really," Matthew, said, but looked evasive.

"What does that mean?"

"Uh, nothing," he said, but turned his head, and glanced away.

"Austin?"

"Uh, not really." His look was sheepish.

"Haley?"

"I'm not going to talk about it," she said; then turned, and left the room.

"It would be nice if he'd given you something," Hannah said. "After all, he's never done much for any of you. Anything to remember him by, or something to make up for everything he didn't give you in the past."

"I wanted his Bible," Haley said, coming back. "I asked, but his wife wouldn't let me have it."

"We weren't supposed to tell you anything," Austin said.

"Why not?" Hannah asked; then stood, and moved to a softer seat.

"Dad told us not to," Matthew said.

"Oh, come on," Hannah said, then, rubbed her hands together, trying to stay calm. "What's the big secret?"

"He said—"

Haley instantly interrupted. "Dad said not to say anything," she said.

"But—"

Again she glared at her brothers. "Remember, Dad said not to tell Mom." Then she put her finger on her lips. "So shhh."

"What's the big secret?" Hannah asked again.

Picking the kids for answers was irresistible. She was still determined to find out, one way or the other. But when she cornered Matthew the following day, a whiff of the truth was revealed. And, as the story unfolded, she realized Jeremy was still using lies to cover himself.

"Dad said your attorney sent him a letter saying not to give us anything," Haley said.

"I don't have an attorney," Hannah said, looking surprised.

Haley turned, and looked her straight in the eye. "He showed us the letter," she said.

'What?" Hannah couldn't help but laugh. "What did it say?" Again she laughed. "After your dad quit paying child support years ago, I gave up on the legal system. Every time I went to court trying to collect what he owed, he always lied to the judge about not having a job. Why would I hire an attorney now? That makes no sense."

"Well, Dad said you'd take legal action if he gave us anything." Matthew was standing his ground.

"I've always wanted him to give you things," Hannah said. "But, he stopped years ago. When was the last time you got a present from him?"

The unease in the room was rising.

"I'll bet you can't even remember the last time."

"But Dad said—" And Austin stood to his feet.

"Your dad pulled the wool over your eyes. He lied to all of you."

"But what about the letter?" Haley asked, then began to pace the floor, holding her head in her hands. "What about that letter?"

"Listen," Hannah said. "I didn't hire an attorney to write a letter to your dad. Like I said before, I've always wanted him to give you things. It would've helped a lot if he did. Instead my money paid for everything—what you wore—the toys you played with. School supplies too. Band instruments—field trips. He never paid for any of it. What about Darren and me paying for this trip so you could see him before he died? What about that?" A long sigh then escaped. "Why would you even think I would do such a thing—hire an attorney so he wouldn't give you anything?"

"Maybe his wife hired the attorney," Matthew said, and then laughed at his own innuendo.

"Maybe she's the one who typed the letter," Austin said. But this suggestion sounded more like the truth than not.

"His wife is a business woman," Hannah said. "Her family owns a workshop business, where your dad worked. She would certainly know how to deal with legal issues."

Her words were starting to take root.

"You know," Haley said, "she kept coming in to see how things were going when we were talking to Dad."

"She probably wrote that letter to make sure you kids didn't get anything after he passed."

He's still telling lies to hide the truth—nothing's changed at all.

"He did give us something," Austin said, then reached for his suitcase. He pulled out a wallet, and opened it. Inside was a crisp fifty-dollar bill.

Here's mine," Matthew said, and reached for his new wallet.

"He gave me fifty dollars too," Haley said, "except mine wasn't in a wallet."

"At least he gave you something," Hannah said, and again sighed.

"Was it worth all that trouble, keeping them from getting something after he died?" Hannah whispered. "I'll never collect the thousands he owes in back child support. So, what's the difference?"

Memories of Jeremy's deception, created by this trip, would remain in Hannah's head a very long time.

Chapter Fifty-Six

Point of View

The events in Hannah's life had been a huge hurdle of conflict and survival. But now was the time for heart and mind to examine the struggle, the what-if's, and the why's of life's journey. So began an intensive time of study, research, and renewal. Volumes of informative material then allowed memories of childhood and first-marriage devastation to collide with Biblical truth and medical knowledge.

Then, over time, understanding and confidence became hers as she learned to appreciate the new life God had blessed her with.

Due to religious beliefs she had been anchored to a marriage that should have ended shortly after it began. But ignorance and pressure from family and church made her a prisoner of her own commitment. Although isolated and uninformed, the desire to provide a safe environment for her children soon became the only focus.

Later, after times of renewal, she began to understand that submission in a marriage does now mean accepting abuse.

As leader in the home, the husband bares the responsibility of love by example. But many refuse to accept their authority in the way it was intended. Often used as an excuse, the man will bully, and literally antagonize, threaten, and attack those placed under his protection and provision—making the scripture, **"Wives, submit** yourselves to your own husbands as you do to the Lord" (Ephesians 5:22) a stumbling block for those who abuse their authority in ways never intended by God. Having control is the deciding factor.

Another truth. Salvage what remains of material goods, and be thankful for what remains. Reclaim what you can, and let go of the rest. Yet understand that some things will never be recoverable. Although difficult to grasp, forgive the one who stole from you. Nothing more can be done, at this point, if the damage is beyond repair. Accept what cannot be changed, and move forward with your life.

Hannah's anchor had always been the Bible—the word of God. Without God on her side, hope for survival, and a better future, would never have been realized.

Although Jeremy retained a fierce passion for preaching the gospel, he also reserved a dark side that manifested in cruelty to animals, as well as family.

It was years following their divorce before Hannah was able to piece together the truth as it was.

In a Nutshell

To the world Hannah was known as the wife of a church pastor. But to the family she was daughter, daughter-in-law, sister-in-law, wife, and mother.

Although memories of her first marriage have faded, the residual of cruel and malicious assaults remain.

Exactly why didn't Hannah leave the marriage when Jeremy began to abuse? Because of church teachings, parental guidance, and in-laws who disapproved of divorce—not to mention that her husband was also the pastor of two churches.

It may sound simple to leave an abusive partner, but it's not. Only after miracles, and years of time, would Hannah again feel safe.

Following their separation, Jeremy continued to stalk, threaten, and terrorize. He often attested that his threat of death was imminent. And, for years, Hannah believed his words.

Symptoms of Multiple Sclerosis also surfaced as did Post-traumatic stress disorder, often referred to as PTSD. Depression and severe panic attacks then enhanced many un-manageable migraines. Still, her escape from abuse has proven every hardship worth the struggle.

"I have been young, and now am old; yet have I not seen the righteous forsaken, nor his seed begging for bread" (Psalms 37:25).

Darren, a profound miracle, has more than enhanced Hannah's life. Today their love remains strong. And, in the process, her children inherited a new father. Although other miracles are part of the equation, the biggest miracle is Darren's unending love.

Till Death Do Us Part—Not

Hannah's parents let her down. The church let her down. The police let her down. Her first marriage let her down. Her in-laws let her down. And, society let her down. But God never *left* her down.

He restored with delight what Satan meant for evil.

"For I know the plans I have for you," declares the LORD, "plans to prosper you and not to harm you, plans to give you hope and a future" (Jeremiah 29:11)

Tribute to a Perfect Husband

Passionate, compassionate, concerned, loving, and gentle; a constant lover in word and deed; a man of his word, integrity his motto, trustworthy, a maintenance man literally and emotionally, a caretaker of both wife and home, loving with every emotion possible from the breadth, depth, and height his soul can reach; a gentleman in every respect of the word, a friend who would lay down his very life if asked; handsome, good-looking, and striking in both tone and stance; and a man who desires his companion at all times.

What more could any woman possibly want?

Chapter Fifty-Seven

Matters of the Heart

Jeremy and Hannah were married **twelve** years. A few years following their divorce he suffered three separate cancers; one after the other. He was forty-three years old when he died—**twelve** years after their divorce.

But her marriage to Darren has lasted over **twenty-four** years.

Many scripture passages in the Bible have proven true, including this one. "I will repay you for the **years** the locusts have eaten" (Job 2:25)

Breast Cancer—Over the Heart

"The heart is deceitful above all things and beyond cure. Who can understand it?" (Jeremiah 17:9)

Brain Tumor—Head of House

"The trouble he causes recoils on himself; their violence comes down on their own **head**s." (Psalms 7:16)

Bone Cancer—Strength
"Because of your (God's) wrath there is no health in his body; there is no soundness in his **bones** because of his sin" (Psalms 38:3)

Breast cancer—issues of the heart
Brain cancer—head of home and church
Leg bone cancer—trampled wife under his feet

***

"Woe **unto the wicked**! It shall be **ill** with him: for **the reward of his hands** shall be given him" (Isaiah 3:11) (KJV)

"Do not be deceived: God cannot be mocked. A **man reaps what he sows**" (Galatians 6:7)

"Though hand join in hand, the wicked shall not be **unpunished**: but the seed of the **righteous shall be delivered**" (Proverbs 11:21) (KJV)

"Dearly beloved, avenge not yourselves, but rather give place unto wrath: for it is written, Vengeance is mine; **I will repay**, saith the Lord," Romans 12: 19) (KJV)

Chapter Fifty-Eight

An Honorable Love Affair

Snuggling closer in Darren's arms, Hannah reached up and gently massaged his labored brow. His hair, now white with age, was soft and yielding to the touch.

Then, as he wrapped his arms around her, she slipped deeper into his warm embrace.

"Tell me again exactly why you married me years ago," she said.

"Because I needed someone to take care of, and you needed someone to care for you—and the kids."

"And—"

He smiled, and then squeezed her hand.

"And that's why God put us together.

"Therefore hath the Lord **recompensed** me according to his righteousness, according to the cleanness of his hands in his eyesight" (Psalms 18:24)

Focused View

I've been lots of places
I thought I'd never go
I've lived a lot of years
Yet life was never slow

I've done a lot of things
I thought I'd never do
I've met many people
But not all have been true

I've given all I've had
To some along the way
The forces of this world
At times led me astray

But as the curve ahead
Comes into focused view
I'll leave it all behind
Save memories of you

© J. Hannah Lloyd

"...To him that overcometh will I give to eat of the hidden manna, and will give him a white stone, and in the stone **a new name** written, which no man knoweth saving he that receiveth it" (Revelations 2:17)

The End

J. HANNAH LLOYD

Acknowledgments

To Ann Tatlock, a personal friend and mentor who helped guide me into the world of professional writing. Without her continual support, this book would not have been written. Our friendship is ongoing, and a testimony of how God works out the details of our lives through others. www.anntatlock.com

To Pamela King Cable, a mentor who provided needed guidance that led to the publishing of this book. She is the author of *Southern Fried Women* and *Televenge—the dark side of televangelism.* www.PamelaKingCable.com

To Pam Zollman, a talented mentor and children's author, speaker, freelance editor, and writing instructor. www.pamzollman.com and www.thewritersplot.com

To Vonda Skelton, a personal friend and mentor, who teaches the fundamentals of basic writing through critique. She is also the Author of *Seeing through the Lies: Unmasking the Myths Women Believe*, and a coveted Conference speaker. www.VondaSkelton.com

J. Hannah Lloyd

About the Author

J. Hannah Lloyd is an author, poet, and free-lance writer who lives near Greenville, South Carolina with her husband and two demanding felines.

In 2007 she was presented two awards for her work at the Blue Ridge Mountain Christian Writer's Conference in Ridgecrest, North Carolina. As a poet and writer her articles, stories, and poetry have enhanced the lives of many; and published in adult and children's Christian literature as well as online. She also contributes poetry bi-monthly to Critter Magazine.

Other works have been published in Slate & Style, Shemom, Harold and Banner Press in Primary Pal: Pacific Press Publishing Association in Our Little Friend, MS Focus and MS Connection Magazines, Who's DANN?—a monthly magazine, Gospel Publishing House in LIVE; a weekly journal; the Pentecostal Evangel—an Assemblies of God publication, Heartland Boating, and the Upper Room magazine.

Visit her online at www.jhannahlloyd.com

Other Books by J. Hannah Lloyd

Escape from Abuse Survival Guide
Ordinary Sayings and Southern Cliché

J. Hannah Lloyd

Proof

Made in the USA
Charleston, SC
26 March 2015